Robert A. Dahl

This book is devoted to the work of Robert A. Dahl, who passed away in 2014. Dahl was one of the most important American political scientists and normative democratic theorists of the post-war era, and he was also an influential teacher who mentored some of the most significant academics of the next two generations of American political science. As an incredibly productive scholar, he had a career that spanned more than half a century: his first book was published in 1950, his last was in 2007 at the age of 92. As a political scientist, he was respected even by those who were critical of his works.

This theoretical significance and profound influence is reflected in the collection of chapters in this volume, which reads like a 'who's who' of the contemporary US political science scene. Among others, this collection includes Dahl's co-author, Bruce Stinebrickner, who documents the evolution of Dahl's thinking as reflected in his seminal text, *Modern Political Analysis*, and describes how it became the standard introduction to American political science for nearly fifty years. Catharine MacKinnon's chapter is of significance for its insights on Dahl and also provides a succinct feminist reading and critique of contemporary political science. Steven Lukes contributes a highly concise statement of the difference between one-dimensional and three-dimensional power.

This work will be a standard reference work for any researchers or those interested in the work of Robert Dahl, among both established academics and students. This book was originally published as a special issue of the *Journal of Political Power*.

David A. Baldwin is a Senior Political Scientist in the Woodrow Wilson School of International and Public Affairs, Princeton University, and Wallach Professor Emeritus, Columbia University. He has contributed articles to *American Political Science Review*, *World Politics*, *Journal of Politics*, *Journal of Conflict Resolution*, and *International Organization*. His most recent book is *Power and International Relations* (Princeton: Princeton University Press, forthcoming).

Mark Haugaard is a Professor of Political Science and Sociology at the National University of Ireland, Galway, Ireland. He is the editor of the *Journal of Political Power*, published by Routledge, and a new book series, *Perspectives on Social and Political Power*, with Manchester University Press. He has published extensively on power, and his most recent publications include 'Concerted Power Over' in *Constellations*, 2015, 22 (1), and 'Two Types of Freedom and Four Dimensions of Power' in *Revue Internationale de Philosophie*, 2016, 70 (275).

Robert A. Dahl
An unended quest

Edited by
David A. Baldwin and Mark Haugaard

LONDON AND NEW YORK

First published 2016
by Routledge
2 Park Square, Milton Park, Abingdon, Oxon, OX14 4RN, UK

and by Routledge
711 Third Avenue, New York, NY 10017, USA

Routledge is an imprint of the Taylor & Francis Group, an informa business

© 2016 Taylor & Francis

All rights reserved. No part of this book may be reprinted or reproduced or utilised in any form or by any electronic, mechanical, or other means, now known or hereafter invented, including photocopying and recording, or in any information storage or retrieval system, without permission in writing from the publishers.

Trademark notice: Product or corporate names may be trademarks or registered trademarks, and are used only for identification and explanation without intent to infringe.

British Library Cataloguing in Publication Data
A catalogue record for this book is available from the British Library

ISBN 13: 978-1-138-65148-7

Typeset in TimesNewRomanPS
by diacriTech, Chennai

Publisher's Note
The publisher accepts responsibility for any inconsistencies that may have arisen during the conversion of this book from journal articles to book chapters, namely the possible inclusion of journal terminology.

Disclaimer
Every effort has been made to contact copyright holders for their permission to reprint material in this book. The publishers would be grateful to hear from any copyright holder who is not here acknowledged and will undertake to rectify any errors or omissions in future editions of this book.

Contents

Citation Information	vii
Notes on Contributors	ix

1. Introduction – Robert A. Dahl: an unended quest   1
   David A. Baldwin and Mark Haugaard

2. Robert Dahl: scholar, teacher, and democrat   11
   Jennifer Hochschild

3. Robert A. Dahl: questions, concepts, proving it   19
   David R. Mayhew

4. Robert A. Dahl and the essentials of *Modern Political Analysis*: politics, influence, power, and polyarchy   33
   Bruce Stinebrickner

5. Misinterpreting Dahl on power   53
   David A. Baldwin

6. Dahl's concept of leadership: notes towards a theory of leadership in a democracy   73
   Nannerl O. Keohane

7. Dahl's feminism?   93
   Catharine A. MacKinnon

8. Robert Dahl on power   105
   Steven Lukes

9. Dahl's power and republican freedom   116
   Philip Pettit

   Index   125

Citation Information

The following chapters were originally published in the *Journal of Political Power*, volume 8, issue 2 (July 2015). When citing this material, please use the original page numbering for each article, as follows:

Chapter 2
Robert Dahl: scholar, teacher, and democrat
Jennifer Hochschild
Journal of Political Power, volume 8, issue 2 (July 2015) pp. 167–174

Chapter 3
Robert A. Dahl: questions, concepts, proving it
David R. Mayhew
Journal of Political Power, volume 8, issue 2 (July 2015) pp. 175–187

Chapter 4
Robert A. Dahl and the essentials of Modern Political Analysis*: politics, influence, power, and polyarchy*
Bruce Stinebrickner
Journal of Political Power, volume 8, issue 2 (July 2015) pp. 189–207

Chapter 5
Misinterpreting Dahl on power
David A. Baldwin
Journal of Political Power, volume 8, issue 2 (July 2015) pp. 209–227

Chapter 6
Dahl's concept of leadership: notes towards a theory of leadership in a democracy
Nannerl O. Keohane
Journal of Political Power, volume 8, issue 2 (July 2015) pp. 229–247

Chapter 7
Dahl's feminism?
Catharine A. MacKinnon
Journal of Political Power, volume 8, issue 2 (July 2015) pp. 249–260

CITATION INFORMATION

Chapter 8
Robert Dahl on power
Steven Lukes
Journal of Political Power, volume 8, issue 2 (July 2015) pp. 261–271

The following chapter was originally published in the *Journal of Political Power*, volume 1, issue 1 (April 2008). When citing this material, please use the original page numbering, as follows:

Chapter 9
Dahl's power and republican freedom
Philip Pettit
Journal of Political Power, volume 1, issue 1 (April 2008) pp. 67–74

For any permission-related enquiries please visit:
http://www.tandfonline.com/page/help/permissions

Notes on Contributors

David A. Baldwin is a Senior Political Scientist in the Woodrow Wilson School of International and Public Affairs, Princeton University, and Wallach Professor Emeritus, Columbia University. He has contributed articles to *American Political Science Review*, *World Politics*, *Journal of Politics*, *Journal of Conflict Resolution*, and *International Organization*. His most recent book is *Power and International Relations* (Princeton: Princeton University Press, forthcoming).

Mark Haugaard is a Professor of Political Science and Sociology at the National University of Ireland, Galway, Ireland. He is the editor of the *Journal of Political Power*, published by Routledge, and a new book series, *Perspectives on Social and Political Power*, with Manchester University Press. He has published extensively on power, and his most recent publications include 'Concerted Power Over' in *Constellations*, 2015, 22 (1), and 'Two Types of Freedom and Four Dimensions of Power' in *Revue Internationale de Philosophie*, 2016, 70 (275).

Jennifer Hochschild is the Henry LaBarre Jayne Professor of Government and Professor of African and African American Studies at Harvard University, USA. Her most recent book (co-authored) is *Do Facts Matter?: Information and Misinformation in American Politics* (2015). She is President-Elect of the American Political Science Association.

Nannerl O. Keohane is a political philosopher who served as president of Wellesley College (1981–1993) and Duke University (1993–2004), and has taught at Swarthmore College, Stanford and Princeton Universities, as well as Wellesley and Duke. Keohane is the author of *Philosophy and the State in France: The Renaissance to the Enlightenment* (1980), *Higher Ground: Ethics and Leadership in the Modern University* (2006), and *Thinking about Leadership* (2010). She is a member of the Harvard Corporation and also on the Board of Trustees of the Doris Duke Charitable Foundation and the Board of Directors of the American Academy of Arts and Sciences. She is currently a Visitor at the Institute for Advanced Study in Princeton, NJ.

Steven Lukes is a Professor of Sociology at New York University, USA. His current research interests include the sociology of morality, and his books include *Emile Durkheim: His Life and Work* (1975), *Individualism* (1978), *Power: A Radical View* (2004), and *Moral Relativism* (2008).

NOTES ON CONTRIBUTORS

Catharine A. MacKinnon is Elizabeth A. Long Professor of Law at the University of Michigan and James Barr Ames Visiting Professor of Law at Harvard Law School (long-term). She holds a BA from Smith College, a JD from Yale Law School, and a PhD in political science from Yale, specializing in sex equality issues in political theory and under international and domestic (including comparative and constitutional) laws. MacKinnon's scholarly books include *Sexual Harassment of Working Women* (1979), *Feminism Unmodified* (1987), *Toward a Feminist Theory of the State* (1989), *Only Words* (1993), *Women's Lives, Men's Laws* (2005), *Are Women Human?* (2006), *Sex Equality* (2001/2007), and *Traite, Prostitution, Inégalité* (2014). Empirical studies document that Professor MacKinnon is among the most widely cited legal scholars in the English language and the most widely cited woman.

David R. Mayhew is Sterling Professor of Political Science at Yale University, USA. He is the author of works on the Congress, parties, elections, policy-making, and political history of the United States, including *Congress: The Electoral Connection* (2005), *Divided We Govern: Party Control, Lawmaking, and Investigations, 1946–2002* (2005), *Electoral Realignments: A Critique of an American Genre* (2004), and *Partisan Balance: Why Political Parties Don't Kill the U.S. Constitutional System* (2011).

Philip Pettit is L.S. Rockefeller University Professor of Politics and Human Values at Princeton University, USA, and Distinguished University Professor of Philosophy at the Australian National University, Australia. His recent works include *The Robust Demands of the Good: Ethics with Attachment, Virtue, and Respect* (2015) and *Just Freedom: A Moral Compass for a Complex World* (2014).

Bruce Stinebrickner is Professor of Political Science at DePauw University, USA. He is the co-author (with Robert A. Dahl) of *Modern Political Analysis*, sixth edition (2003), and has published articles on the American presidential selection process, public policy addressing children, American state and local governments, and the career patterns of Australian politicians. He is also the editor of 38 editions of *American Government* and 16 editions of *State and Local Government* in McGraw-Hill's Annual Editions series of books.

Introduction
Robert A. Dahl: an unended quest

David A. Baldwin[a] and Mark Haugaard[b]

[a]Columbia and Princeton University, USA; [b]National University of Ireland, Galway, Ireland

The legacy of Robert A. Dahl

The following essays are devoted to the work of Robert A. Dahl (1915–2014), whose immensely productive scholarly career spanned more than half a century. His first book was published in 1950 and his last in 2007 at the age of 92. During these years, he published numerous articles and more than twenty books. After spending his entire academic career as a member of the Department of Political Science at Yale University, he retired in 1986 and served thereafter as Sterling Professor Emeritus of Political Science and Senior Research Scientist in Sociology at Yale.

Professor Dahl served as President of the American Political Science Association in 1967, as a member of the National Academy of Sciences, the American Philosophical Society, the American Academy of Arts and Sciences, and as a corresponding member of the British Academy. In 1995, he was the first recipient of the Johan Skytte Prize in Political Science, an award given by Uppsala University in Sweden to the scholar who has made the most valuable contribution to political science.

It is impossible here to consider the many contributions Dahl made to the study of politics. We shall therefore consider only four—as political scientist, as methodologist, as power analyst, and as democratic theorist.

As a political scientist, he was respected even by those who were critical of his works. The *Yale Daily News* (February 7, 2014) noted that *Foreign Affairs* had called him the 'dean of American political scientists.' And his student and colleague, Ian Shapiro, observed that 'he might well have been the most important political scientist of the last century, and he was certainly one of its preeminent social scientists.' Shapiro added that:

> In many ways, Dahl created the field of modern political science. To be sure, the scholarly study of politics goes back to at least the ancient Greeks. Dahl was no Plato, Aristotle, or Thomas Hobbes; but he added something new to the armchair reflection leavened by illuminating anecdote that characterized the enterprise for millennia: the systematic use of evidence to evaluate rigorously stated theoretical claims. Generations of Dahl's successors have developed both theories and empirical methods in multiple directions since he produced his innovative works in the 1950s and 1960s, sometimes in ways that he found less than congenial. Few would deny that they stood on Dahl's shoulders (Shapiro, 2014).

ROBERT A. DAHL

Despite Dahl's contributions to empirical political science, it would be a mistake to describe him as nothing but an empiricist. He also recognized—and practiced—normative inquiry and conceptual analysis as important components of modern political analysis. Various works as well as his text *Modern Political Analysis* make this clear. Nor can his work be described in terms of a single subfield of political science. As Jeffrey Isaac points out:

> [Dahl] wrote major books that were seminal to three subfields of political science— 'A Preface to Democratic Theory' (political theory), 'Who Governs?' (American politics), and 'Polyarchy' (comparative politics). Indeed his work straddled and bridged the conventional subfields, none of which could encompass his thinking (2014).

In addition to the subfields identified by Isaac, one could mention the seminal contribution to the relatively new subfield of political economy he co-authored with Charles E. Lindblom—*Politics, Economics, and Welfare* (1953). In 1997, he observed that the book was a response to the need:

> To recreate a modern 'political economy,' after the late nineteenth-century divorce of neoclassical economics and political science. Scholars who specialized in politics were (and too often still are) woefully ignorant of economic theory, and neoclassical economists were (and too many still are) ignorant about and disdainful of political life (1997, p. 6).

As a methodologist, Dahl's name is associated with the 'behavioral movement' in political science in the 1950s and 1960s. The three components of this movement were (1) increased emphasis on empirical research, (2) more methodological self-consciousness, and (3) establishing links with other behavioral sciences—sociology, psychology, anthropology, and economics. Although he was a leader—perhaps *the* leader—of the behavioral movement, he was never a captive thereof. The following passage makes this unmistakably clear:

> Some readers of my work may not fully appreciate that different problems require different methodologies or a different mix of methodologies. I have never felt that any particular methodology or approach is inherently superior to others. What is best depends on the question, the problem. Historical, behavioral, quantitative, linguistic, moral-ethical, and institutional methods and approaches all have a place, though not necessarily in the same work. Methodologically speaking, I am deliberately and shamelessly eclectic. I believe strongly that the question one wants to investigate should dictate the choice of methodology; a methodology should never dictate the choice of question (1997, p. 8).

As a power analyst, Dahl set out to bring clarity and precision to what he saw as an unsatisfactory treatment of the concept of power in social science. He described himself as having been 'dismayed by the casual and undiscriminating way in which most social scientists, including political scientists, employed the term "power," ignoring the complexities of the concept as if somehow these complexities were trivial' (1997, p. 12). He identifies Thomas Hobbes, Max Weber, and Harold Lasswell as important influences on his thinking about power. For Dahl, power was the essential defining

ROBERT A. DAHL

characteristic of politics. And since he saw power as ubiquitous, he viewed politics in many social relations not commonly thought of as 'political'—including romantic couples, churches, business firms, families, and even academic departments.

Most (perhaps all) of Dahl's work relates directly or indirectly to democracy. He notes, however, that 'I never set out to become a "democratic theorist." Even the term "democratic theory" hardly existed when I began writing.' Looking back nearly forty years later, Dahl described his first book, *Congress and Foreign Policy* (1950), as 'really a venture in "democratic theory," though I probably would not have put it that way in 1950' (1997, p. 6). Dahl not only became a 'democratic theorist,' he came to be widely viewed as the founder of this field of study. The term 'polyarchy,' first introduced by Dahl and Lindblom in 1953, has become an essential part of contemporary democratic theory.

Reflections upon the essays in this collection

It is striking that all the authors in this collection have a profound intellectual respect for Robert Dahl and many, especially those that knew him personally, felt a deep fondness for him as an individual. These fine qualities are not two different elements but are intertwined.

This phenomenon is most immediately felt in Dahl's use of prose. Dahl crafted words upon the page in such a way that readers have the sensation that the author is speaking directly to them. This is similar to the way great portrait painters can make the subject on the canvas so alive that you feel them looking at you.

The sensation of a living voice is particularly strong in Dahl's use of Socratic dialogue. In *Democracy and Its Critics* (1989), Dahl becomes the wise, kindly, interlocutor arguing on behalf of pluralist democracy, against the challenges of Anarchos (Dahl, 1989, pp. 39–41) and Aristos (1989, pp. 55–64). While Dahl argues with conviction, what makes him particularly effective is that he is also a good listener. When Dahl speaks on behalf of Anarchos or Aristos, he puts their best arguments forward to test and then refute them, but never in a dismissive way. Dahl does not set up straw men to be demolished. Rather, Dahl is listening and openly acknowledges that his adversaries (especially Aristos) have powerful arguments.

This openness to other points of view applies both to Robert Dahl's published work and to his interaction with others, as related in an anecdote narrated to us by Jennifer Hochschild in her essay.

Hochschild is deeply appreciative of Dahl's work in its widest sense, which includes his role as mentor and teacher. However, she is critical of the fact that *race* is not sufficiently prominent in Dahl's early work. In one particular essay, Dahl lists five periods of consequential expansion of the democratic decision-making process in the United States, but fails to include among these the abolition of slavery. However, when she queried this omission to him in person, Dahl readily volunteered that he wished he were in a position to retrospectively rewrite that article in order to correct his mistake.

Dahl's ability to listen and rethink his position is not simply about quality of character. It links into his wider scientific interpretative world-view, which was not black and white. Rather, it was nuanced shades of gray. Unlike many of his intellectual interlocutors, Dahl's version of democracy is an imperfect thing. Dahl is clear about the various attributes that a democracy should aspire to, yet he appreciates that no democracy can ever fully reach these ideals. Real-life pluralist democracy, or polyarchy, is an imperfect thing but desirable nonetheless.

Dahl's normative world was a scalar one, with tyranny at one end and the egalitarian ideals of democracy at the other. Real-life democracies, as they happen in the actual empirical world, are somewhere on that scale. Over the course of his life, we see Dahl's placement of US democracy slips further from the ideal end of the scale, toward the midway point.

Dahl's generosity of spirit, which was refracted through nuanced shades of gray scalar vision, is linked to a wider methodological orientation. Dahl combines a Weberian use of ideal types with a scientific, Popperian (Popper, 1992) type, quest for falsification.

As argued by David Mayhew in this book, Dahl's use of ideal types is both empirical and normative. On the empirical level, this means that Dahl distils the essence of a phenomenon into clear concepts that serve as conceptual tools to order the world in a systematic way. Normatively, the use of ideal types means theorizing the evaluative aspirations of democracy. Neither empirical concepts nor normative ideals are to be found in their pure form in the empirical world.

The emphasis upon scientific method combined with the empirical ideal types gives Dahl the reflective capacity to begin all his analysis with the right questions. As argued by Mayhew, one of the reasons that Dahl stands out as a scholar is that he always begins his research with the right questions. For instance, the opening sentence of *Who Governs?* ('In a political system where nearly every adult may vote but where knowledge, wealth, social position, access to officials, and other resources are unequally distributed, who actually governs?' [1961, p. 1]) represents the key question for anyone who wishes to empirically test the level of democracy of a system.

Theorizing by constructing ideal types means simplifying the world. You reach the essence of something by removing what is considered extraneous. When Galileo wanted to understand the falling movement of bodies, he theorized this by methodologically bracketing the resistance of air. That was despite the fact that Galileo could only test his ideas by performing experiments surrounded by air. This simplification entails the exclusion of what is *judged* to be extraneous.

As argued by Hochschild in this book, in this respect Dahl's conceptual strength could manifest itself as his weakness. While *Who Governs?* is a seminal text of empirical rigor, it also contains a remarkable lack, which is a blindness to the significance of race. It is not that race was entirely absent, or that Dahl had, in any way, a racial bias. Rather, Dahl failed to see that the urban redevelopment of New Haven was also the beginning of a black/white ghettoization that would, not many years after the study, transform itself into overt racial tensions. In short, through the process of scientific simplification of the data, Dahl had excluded a key variable that, with the benefit of hindsight, turned out to be significant.

The use of empirically based ideal types made Dahl careful in defining his concepts. He used these conceptual tools with remarkable skill. As argued by Bruce Stinebrickner in his essay, spanning four decades of Dahl's scholarly career, Dahl framed the language of contemporary political science. His 1957 article is the beginning of real scientific, as opposed to polemical, debate on the nature and distribution of power.

In his essay, Stinebrickner traces the evolution of Dahl's development of concepts through careful analysis of the development of the various editions of *Modern Political Analysis* (*MPA*), from its first edition in 1963 to the sixth in 2003 (Dahl and Stinebrickner 1963—Stinebrickner was the co-author of the latter but, modestly, treats this work as entirely Dahl's).

The first edition *MPA* definition of the essence of *politics* was exceptionally forward-looking. Dahl defined politics in terms of the exercise of *influence*. This was a much wider definition than any of his contemporaries and predecessors, who tended to equate politics with government or control of territory. This makes Dahl's conceptualization of *politics* still relevant in the contemporary context in which, for instance, feminists, such as Catharine MacKinnon, would argue that the family constitutes a part of the political sphere.

As argued by Stinebrickner, having defined politics in terms of influence, Dahl points out that although influence terms are central to political analysis, they are rarely properly defined. It is from this premise that we obtain his renowned definitions of the vocabulary of power, which include not only his previous definition of power ('A has power over B to the extent that he can get B to do something that B would not otherwise do' [1957, p. 202]) but also the distinction between the exercise of power and power resources, scope and domain of power, and other influence terms, including inducement, force, coercion, persuasion, manipulation, and authority.

As *MPA* develops over the six editions, Dahl absorbs some of the criticisms made of his work on power. In the sixth edition, he distinguishes four levels of decision-making. As set out by Stinebrickner, these include (1) conflict within the options of an already existing agenda, (2) changes to the agenda, (3) structures, and (4) the awareness of social actors. Stinebrickner views this four-level framework as Dahl's *last word* in response to his many critics in the three-dimensional power debate, including Steven Lukes.

It is a debatable point whether this response actually represents a shift in position or simply a clarification of a relatively constant position. In his essay, David Baldwin argues that much of the (so-called) three- (or four-) dimensional power debate entails attributing ideas and concepts to Dahl that he did not hold. For instance, as also observed by Stinebrickner, Dahl never linked power to interests, so in that sense his perspective was wider than Lukes'. Unlike Dahl, in the first edition of *Power: A Radical View* (1974), Lukes defines power in terms of the inability of the dominated to realize their *interests*; while in the second edition (2005) and his contribution to this book, Lukes acknowledges that this was too narrow. Power is neutral with regard to the subject of B's interests, which it was for Dahl from the very beginning.

The conventional rendering of this debate (whereby Dahl begins with a narrow one-dimensional view and others widen the concept through the addition of other dimensions) is fundamentally flawed because it is based upon a failure to understand the full implications of using Weberian ideal types. Ideal-type concepts are constructed through a distillation of the essence of the empirical world. Consequently, these conceptual constructions do not exist empirically in the pure form. Hence, when dealing with a particular empirical project, such as measuring power in New Haven, it can be necessary to use operational definitions that are of a lower order, closer to reality, than the ideal types.

As argued by Baldwin, there is a significant gap between ideal-type concepts and operational definitions created for specific purposes. For the purposes of the empirical analysis undertaken to write *Who Governs?* it may be operationally necessary to measure power in terms of decision-making. However, this is not equivalent to claiming that the concept of power solely equates to decision-making. Consequently, it is not inconsistent to measure power in terms of decision-making while acknowledging that, for instance, the notables of New Haven had power by virtue of a collectively shared sense of the legitimacy of the power of old patrician families (contrary to Lukes [2005, p. 27]). To use Bourdieu's conceptual vocabulary, this collective sense is part of the *habitus* of the community, which constitutes cultural capital for these old families. This *habitus*, and associated cultural capital, constitutes an example of Lukes' third dimension of power, which may well be compatible with Dahl's wider concept of power, although not with his operational definition.

Dahl's methodological specificity entails that some important power and democracy related phenomena did not always receive the treatment they may have deserved. This was not necessarily an exclusion or omission, rather a task still to be undertaken. Nowhere in his writings is there a systematic analysis of *leadership*. Yet throughout his work there are discussions of the subject. In her essay, Nannerl O. Keohane brings these discussions together in order to frame her reconstruction of Dahl's concept of leadership.

Leadership emerges as a subtle and complex category nested at the core of Dahl's concept of democracy and power. For Dahl, the impossibility of democracy to reach its normative ideals is not simply due to the imperfections of real life. Rather, in this case, it is for structural reasons. Once we move into complex societies, it is impossible for ordinary citizens to devote the time necessary to politics. These practical complexities require leaders who devote themselves full-time to politics. This pragmatic necessity entails a move away from the normative ideals of democracy. However, unlike elitists or socialists, for whom democracy is an either/or phenomenon, Dahl's more nuanced, shades of gray, scalar democracy has conceptual space for leaders, who by virtue of their actions can be characterized as more or less democratic.

Democratic leadership is not simply a question of good personality. A structural force that works in favor of democratic (as opposed to despotic) leadership is the desire of most leaders to stabilize their political power in terms of the discourse of legitimate authority. They accomplish this by dressing up their actions in the rhetoric and rituals of the will of the people, rather than their own will. Hence, there is a certain pragmatism which militates in favor of democracy. Consequently, leadership emerges as a complex category, which points both ways in terms of democratic normative aspirations.

When framing a scientific analysis, there is not only the question of the way the frame includes and excludes but also the way in which certain phenomena appear under that frame. We saw that *race* was not sufficiently visible in *Who Governs?* There

ROBERT A. DAHL

is also another aspect to this phenomenon. Following Thomas Kuhn's (1970, 1977) account of paradigms, it is not only what data are visible but *how* (in what way) they are made visible that is crucial.

As argued by Catharine A. MacKinnon, even back in the 1950s, Dahl was highly conscious of the way in which women are dominated. In his writings, women *are visible* and never appear just as an afterthought. So in that regard the theorization of women is unlike that of race. However, in terms of interpretation, the place of women within the democratic process appears largely framed with reference to the issue of inclusion. The story runs something likes this: in early US democracy, the enfranchised included only middle-class white males, then working-class males, and then blacks and women. This theorization assumes an interpretation of women's domination solely in terms of exclusion. However, as argued by MacKinnon, if we consider women's domination in terms of male violence, which is reproduced in the family, then female domination appears a paradigmatically different phenomenon. The state that protects these institutions through law becomes the embodiment of violence against half the population.

This paradigmatic interpretative quality also extends to other phenomena. We have already seen that in the sixth edition of *MPA*, Dahl answers his critics by widening the concept of power to include influencing the awareness of social actors. Yet it can be argued that what Dahl meant by this is slightly different from the paradigmatic meaning of Lukes' third dimension of power. In his article, Lukes critiques the idea, set out by Stinebrickner, that Dahl had the *final word* on power in the sixth edition of *MPA*, and Baldwin's arguments to the effect that the interpreters of Dahl attributed to him views of power that were much narrower than was in fact the case.

Lukes argues that Dahl's 1957 perception of power and influence as equivalents, and his attendant A versus B definition, are in fact so wide that this concept of power needs refining to be useful. This act of refinement gives you the *conception* that covers the essence of the *concept*. This is slightly different from an operational definition (Baldwin), which is simply a conceptual tool for a specific, often empirical, task. To take a parallel, justice as fairness is Rawls' concept of justice, but his principles are the conception. Lukes argues that, while the concept is wide, the conception of power implicit in *Who Governs?* is too narrow. As for the so-called (by Stinebrickner) *final word* of the sixth edition of *MPA*, Lukes acknowledges that the underlying conception is wider but still not wide enough.

Speaking more generally, one of the issues underlying the debate between Dahl and Lukes is the significance of the background (often unintended) structural and epistemic conditions of social interaction. Even though the *MPA* analysis includes both knowledge and structure, the point is that as long as this is linked to the *exercise* of power, the ways in which these background conditions shape the power dispositions is lost. Following Morriss (2002), for Lukes power is a dispositional concept and, as a consequence, need not be wielded by the powerful.

The three-dimensional power debate entails the wider phenomenon of the tacit knowledge, or *habitus*, that frames a society's perceptions of the conditions of the possible and reasonable. To use an example (editors' example), before women had the franchise, the obstacles to full democracy were not simply one of men exercising

ROBERT A. DAHL

power over women, or agenda setting, or of influencing women's wants in some clever way. The relations of domination were sustained because that whole natural 'order of things' was interpreted in essentialist terms. Essentialism was how pre-modern natural scientists made sense of the movements of the heavens, so it was entirely logical that society as a whole (not just men), according to their *habitus*, conceived of human relations in essentialist terms. Essentialism was not only central to legitimating male–female relations: it was a tacit assumption that made many class distinctions appear natural. It was part of the vocabulary of legitimation of the differential dispositions of social actors. In that indirect sense, overthrowing the essentialist paradigm was part of the democratic process in a deep (second nature) mode of social critique and change. Thus, the third dimension of power is not simply about what the powerful do, how they exercise their power, but entails attention to the everyday epistemic constitution of the interpretative horizon of everyday life.

Against this critique, it could be argued that Dahl was highly conscious of the epistemic foundations of democracy. Following de Tocqueville, Dahl was always fascinated by the conditions of possibility of democracy. So, we can extrapolate that Dahl's methodological canvas could be extended to include this phenomenon.

Lukes' critique of Dahl draws our attention to contextuality of social action, including the capacity to shape a person's wants and desires. This focus is given an unusual twist in Philip Pettit's contribution. This essay (which was first published in the *Journal of Power* 1.1. in 2008) constitutes an engagement with Dahl's concept of power, relative to the republican concept of freedom. In particular, Pettit argues that potential power, which is never exercised, can have a dominating effect. Consequently, republican theory requires that we should make sure not to confine our understanding of domination purely to the exercise of power.

Pettit puts this in terms of moving beyond a punctualist, or point in time, view of power. In order to explain why Pettit's republicanism requires this expanded emphasis, we will refer to Pettit's analyses of the relationship between Nora and Torvald in Ibsen's play *A Doll's House*, which is analyzed in *Just Freedom* (Pettit, 2014, pp. xii–xviii). Torvald is a kind husband who denies his wife nothing. However, according to the laws and norms of the time, Torvald has the *potential* power to interfere with Nora's life in a manner uncongenial to her interests. The fact that Torvald never actually exercises his dominating power resources does not alter the fact that Nora's freedom exists with the permission, thus at the whim, of Torvald. This is freedom as a contingent fact. In contrast, in republican normative theory, the freedom of a citizen is based upon legal entitlement. Consequently, even if there is no point in time when Torvald uses his power to limit the freedom of Nora, the possession of unequal potential power is inimical to her freedom.

As a comment, we would argue that the exercise perception of power, which is attributed to Dahl, was specifically developed as part of a set of measures of levels of democracy. For Dahl, democracy constitutes a set of structures created for the purposes of implementing equality in decision-making (Dahl, 1989, pp. 83–96). Consequently, when measuring the level of democracy in New Haven (Dahl 1961), it makes sense to emphasize decision-making. While Pettit's republicanism requires democratic political structures (thus is compatible with Dahl's vision), Pettit's republican endeavor is different in emphasis. His starting point is not equality or decision-making, but freedom (hence the title of the book *Just Freedom* [2014]). Republican freedom is wider in scope than equality in decision-making, and includes within it a normative evaluation of what it means to be an agent, as a full citizen. Consequently, the difference in objective between measuring democratic equality and republican freedom entails the reformulation of conceptual tools.

If we think of Dahl's work as a set of conceptual tools that can be used, then the analysis of power is not something set in stone, but a living language, which forms and re-forms according to theoretical need. Therefore, as is implied by Pettit, it is not a fundamental critique of Dahl to argue that his language of power has to be expanded, reformed, or retooled in order to move from the language of democratic equality to Pettit's account of republican freedom. In fact, it is a tribute to Dahl's perspicacity that the conceptual tools that he has bequeathed to us can be reformed in this manner—they live on.

In conclusion, Robert Dahl was a great thinker, the potentials of whose work we are still exploring. His work was for him, and is for us, an unended quest.

Acknowledgement
The editors would like to acknowledge the contribution of Jeffrey Isaac to organizing the special issue and this book. Although he had to withdraw from further participation for health reasons, his initial encouragement and advice were immensely helpful.

References
Dahl, R.A., 1950. *Congress and Foreign Policy*. New York: W.W. Norton.
Dahl, R.A., 1957. The concept of power. *Behavioral Science*, 2(3), 201–215.
Dahl, R.A., 1961. *Who Governs? Democracy and Power in an American City*. New Haven, CT: Yale University Press.
Dahl, R.A., 1963. *Modern Political Analysis*. Englewood Cliffs, NJ: Prentice-Hall.
Dahl, R.A., 1989. *Democracy and Its Critics*, New Haven, CT: Yale University Press, New Haven.
Dahl, R.A., 1997. *Toward Democracy: A Journey, Reflections: 1940–1997*. Berkeley: Institute of Governmental Studies Press and University of California.
Dahl, R.A. and Lindblom, C.E., 1953. *Politics, Economics, and Welfare*. New York: Harper & Row.
Dahl, R.A. and Stinebrickner, B., 2003. *Modern Political Analysis*. 6th edn. Upper Saddle River, NJ: Prentice-Hall.
Isaac, J., 2014. 'Robert Dahl as mentor.' www.washingtonpost.com/blogs/monkey-cage/wp/2014/02/11/robert-dahl-as-mentor.
Kuhn, Thomas S., 1970. *The Structure of Scientific Revolutions*. Chicago: The University of Chicago Press.
Kuhn, Thomas S., 1977. *The Essential Tension: Selected Studies in Scientific Thought and Change*. Chicago: The University of Chicago Press.
Lukes, S., 1974. *Power: A Radical View*. London: Macmillan.
Lukes, S., 2005. *Power: A Radical View*. 2nd edn. Basingstoke: Palgrave Macmillan, Houndsmills.

ROBERT A. DAHL

Morriss, P., 2002. *Power: A Philosophical Analysis*. 2nd edn. Manchester: Manchester University Press.

Pettit, P., 2008. 'Dahl's power and republican freedom.' *Journal of [Political] Power*, 1(1): 67–74.

Pettit, P., 2014. *Just Freedom: A Moral Compass for a Complex World*. New York: W.W. Norton.

Popper, K., 1992. *The Logic of Scientific Discovery*. London: Routledge.

Shapiro, I., 2014. 'Democracy man: the life and work of Robert A. Dahl.' *Foreign Affairs*, February, 12. https://www.foreignaffairs.com/articles/2014-02-12/democracy-man

Robert Dahl: scholar, teacher, and democrat

Jennifer Hochschild

Department of Government, CGIS, Harvard University, Cambridge, USA

Robert Dahl's greatness as a political scientist rested on three qualities: the analytic clarity of his definitions of democracy, his insistence on studying complex ideas such as 'power' in a systematic empirical manner, and his commitment to a moral or normative underpinning for one's scholarship. He was a deep egalitarian intellectually and interpersonally. However, many of Dahl's publications had a considerable blindspot; until late in life, he did not fully recognize how much racial hierarchy and discrimination undermined his and others' claims that the United States has a reasonably well functioning and robust democracy. This blind spot teaches us to be intellectually humble, to recognize the defects of even the strongest methodological strategies, and to recognize our own mistakes, as Dahl did.

Like so many of his students and colleagues, I am proud and even grateful (a term we do not use much) to describe Robert Dahl as a teacher, intellectual model, and eventually friend.[1] His was a life of civic and political activity, transformative scholarship, influential teaching, university leadership, and an overall level of integrity and decency that few people – perhaps especially, few scholars – can match. This journal issue attests to Dahl's importance, as did the broad public attention to his death. And for good reason: he exemplified the democratic citizen and did more than perhaps any other writer in the last half of the twentieth century to shape debates over what democracy is and should be.

Dahl's body of work influenced my generation of political scientists so deeply that it is hard to sort out where his impact lay; we breathe his air. Let me first describe his intellectual strengths, then examine one notable flaw. Both are illuminating.

The first striking feature of Dahl's work is analytic. He taught us how to think about what a political system needs in order to be democratic, different ways a society might organize itself and still plausibly be democratic, and how components of a democracy work together or stymie one another. A democratic political system might follow James Madison's constitutional logic, in which powerful groups and institutions offset one another so that no faction gets too much control and so that the government has little chance of accruing too much power (the high school civics notion of checks and balances, or 'ambition countering ambition' in Madison's words). Alternatively, a democratic political system might be populist, making it

ROBERT A. DAHL

easier for majorities to get their way in policy design and implementation, but risking threats to the rights or interests of minorities.

Or, in the definition that Dahl preferred, a genuine democracy must have the social arrangements and norms that enable all people to participate and all groups and ideas to compete freely and fairly. That implies some stringent conditions – freedom of movement, speech, and association; a robust press or other channels of information; frequent, free, and fair elections with genuine alternatives; sufficient resources held by members of the public so they are free to think and act as they please; limits on the potentially overweening power of corporations and other huge organizations, and more. As his radicalism deepened through his career and as he grew more disillusioned about the workings of governments, Dahl eventually declined to call any existing political system a democracy. Since no actual society has sufficient participation and effective contestation, even the most admirable only rise to the level of being polyarchies (Dahl 1971).

That point implies another crucial element of Dahl's research and teaching: One must carefully study what is actually happening in governance to determine how democratic a city or country really is. If that seems self-evident, it is because we are so influenced by Dahl's writing. Before his most famous book, *Who Governs?* (Dahl 2005 [1961]), much scholarship on democracy focused on constitutional structures, laws and formal procedures, or theories of class domination. Too often, an argument received support mainly from anecdotes, historical analogies, deep conviction, sheer ego, or narrowly construed investigations.

In contrast, Dahl and a few other scholars promoted a systematic behavioral revolution-turned-mainstream (Dahl 1961). He and his students chose the small city of New Haven for a case study, immersing themselves in the minutiae of how a mayor and his associates govern: Who gets to choose the next aldermanic candidates? Who gets to decide where the housing project will be built? What does the school board do? How does a leader acquire or lose influence? How do a city's Notables interact with its Plebes, both in one period and over generations or even centuries? Power, in this view, does not exist unless one can observe and enumerate A getting B to do something that B would not otherwise do – none of this airy nonsense about penumbras, potential influence, unspoken control, or mental domination (Dahl 1957, Dahl 1958).

I teach *Who Governs?* as the first book in my favorite course, on 'Power in American Society'. The smart and assertive students love to tear into it, showing how it is naïve, incomplete, outdated, insufficiently rigorous, and complacent. But the careful readers among them come to see that Dahl anticipated and dealt with most of their objections. They discover how difficult it is to refute his core assertion that a reasonably well-functioning political system can give everyone the opportunity to have at least a little political impact. Above all, *Who Governs?* shows what one can do when a powerful analytic theory about the meaning of democracy is unobtrusively melded into a careful, even pedantic-seeming, study of politics on the ground.

Dahl's implicit call for a moral or normative underpinning for one's research was the final crucial element of his impact. He was both an instinctive and an intentional egalitarian, reverting to the radicalism of his youth as he grew older. By the 1980s, while a majority of Americans were moving to the political and economic right, Dahl became more and more insistent that without much greater material equality, political equality was impossible. He asserted, for example, the necessity of workers' ownership or control of large firms: '*if* democracy was justified in governing the state, then it must *also* be justified in governing economic enterprises; and to say that it is *not* justified in governing economic enterprises is to imply that it is not justified in governing the state'. This was published at the mid-point of the Reagan presidency.

Near the end of his life, Dahl once again explored the meaning of equality and its centrality to any democratic project. In arguably his strongest prose ever (Dahl 2003), he excoriated the American Constitution for creating a political structure that denies equal participation and contestation to all citizens. He called on Americans to rethink the conditions necessary for a genuine democracy, compared the United States unfavorably with other polyarchies, and proposed his own constitutional and statutory reform. Intellectually at least, he did not go gently into that good night.

Because what I see as Dahl's major scholarly flaw is so closely linked to his singular virtues, I now turn to an examination of one important blind spot in his body of writing. Despite his commitment to equality and the dignity of all, many publications were insufficiently attentive to the most serious failure of American democracy – its history of slavery, apartheid, and arguably continued second-class citizenship of many African Americans. *Who Governs?* and perhaps my favorite of his essays, 'On Removing Certain Impediments to Democracy in the United States' (Dahl 1977), both demonstrate this blind spot, and also provide lessons from which all scholars can benefit.

The first quarter of *Who Governs?* examines the transition in political power from the patricians of the late eighteenth century to the ex-plebes, 'rising out of the working-class or lower middle-class families of immigrant origin', by the middle of the twentieth century. 'This change – one might properly call it a revolution – appears to be a profound alteration in the ways political resources are distributed among the citizens of New Haven'. It created an all-important 'shift from cumulative inequalities ... to noncumulative or dispersed inequalities' (all quotations in this paragraph on p. 11). The rest of the book traces the ways in which these dispersed inequalities create a rough-and-ready democracy (what Dahl might later have characterized as a local polyarchy). Citizens can attain at least a small share of political power if they try hard enough, they can influence a crucial policy decision if they organize and expend slack resources, they can have an impact on one or another arena of governance. Citizens are linked by a shared belief in democratic norms and practices that exercise crucial restraints on power-holders even when more honored in the breach than in the observance. Overall, this is a reasonably optimistic, gratifying portrayal of inevitably flawed people and institutions behaving decently and fairly.

And yet, published in 1961, *Who Governs?* almost completely missed the racial dynamics of New Haven, a city that exploded in riots and protests a few years later. Index entries provide an artificial but telling indicator of the book's attention. 'Ethnic' has eight entries, many with multiple pages, and the index entry further directs the reader to 'See also Germans, Irish, Italians, ... Russians [and Immigration]' – each of which identifies an additional set of up to a dozen entries. By comparison, the ellipsis in the previous sentence directs the reader to 'Negroes', which offers five entries.

More revealing than a simple count is the way in which *Who Governs?* generally points to racial issues. 'Race' or 'racial' appears several times in the index, but

ROBERT A. DAHL

almost always the entry points to a list that includes other societal divisions. For example:

- 'member of a particular interest group, social stratum, neighborhood, race, ethnic group, or profession' (p. 93);
- 'Nor have I seen any issues that you could call racial or religious issues', in a quotation from 'an unusually tough-minded informant' (p. 149);
- 'social standing, religion, ethnic origin, or racial stock' (p. 226);
- 'That regional, ethnic, racial, religious, or economic differences might disrupt the American political system has been a recurring fear among the political stratum' (p. 318).

Dahl quotes a sociologist on the 'socio-biological axis of race' in New Haven, with 'two social worlds ... – a Negro world and a white world'. This expert's revealing start continues, however, by exploring divisions among whites, and says nothing more about Negroes (p. 234). Dahl does not comment or add his own gloss.

A caveat is essential here. *Who Governs?* does point to race-based discrimination; in almost the last chapter, Dahl observes that 'probably the most significant group in New Haven whose opportunities are sharply restricted by social and economic barriers are Negroes' (p. 293). He points to residential segregation – 'although they are gradually dispersing' – employment discrimination – although 'discrimination is declining' – and poverty (p. 293). But *Who Governs?* turns away from racial hierarchy after a few paragraphs, developing instead, with data analyzed over several pages, an argument that 'in local politics and government the barriers are comparatively slight'. Negroes vote and are more politically active than comparable whites, they are the objects of party competition, they suffer no discrimination in public employment, and they always have a representative on the Board of Aldermen and in one city-wide office.

In short, race (by which Dahl usually though not always meant a difference between all blacks and all whites) and racial hierarchy certainly appear in *Who Governs?* But with rare exceptions, race plays no distinct role in the narrative; as the index entries and lists above show, the division between blacks and whites usually has the same or even less linguistic and analytic status as the division between Irish and Italians or between Protestants and Catholics. More deeply, Dahl's central agenda in *Who Governs?* is to show the political implications of the 'revolution' that occurred with the dispersal of resources from the patricians to the ex-plebes. The book's underlying contention is that, although social, economic, political inequalities persisted in the late 1950s, they were not structural, rigid, or impermeable. In that way, New Haven could reasonably be understood to represent 'democracy itself' (p. xv).

Urban redevelopment was one of Dahl's three case studies for determining who actually governs, and it could have been the setting for probing the racially biased features of New Haven's politics and policy-making. But it was not. Given redevelopment's status as 'the central policy of his [Mayor Lee's] administration' (p. 121), Dahl attends carefully to the creation and maintenance of a favorable political coalition, and shows how this policy initiative reinforced Lee's power and capacity for leadership. His purpose, that is, was 'not an appraisal of the desirability of the program but an attempt to understand the political forces that shaped it'

(p. 115). Thus although Dahl points out that 'by 1959 much of the center of the city was razed to the ground', he never hints at the viewpoint that became prominent a few years later, of urban renewal as 'Negro removal'.

We need more context to make sense of Dahl's treatment of race and urban renewal. On the one hand, Negroes were 'a relatively small though increasing minority', comprising less than 10% of the population and concentrated in only a few wards (p. 293). Irish and Italian ethnics were much more numerous and much more consequential to New Haven's politics and policy-making. And almost no one with political influence or public visibility perceived a racial problem in northern cities before the 1960s; virtually everyone during the 1950s perceived job or housing discrimination to be private issues. To my knowledge, no prominent political actor pointed out in the 1950s that the razing of 'slums' might make their residents worse off than before, reinforcing blacks' segregation, powerlessness, and alienation. In fact, as Dahl points out, one of Mayor Lee's 'action committees' set up to promote redevelopment 'was made up in great measure of social workers, liberals, clergymen, Negro leaders, housing officials, and religious leaders' (p. 134).

On the other hand, the black population in New Haven was indeed increasing, and rapidly. African Americans comprised 5.8% of the city's population in 1950, 14.5% in 1960, and 26.3% in 1970.[2] And racial dynamics looked very different a few years after *Who Governs?* was published: 'the late 1960s were chaotic in New Haven, CT. Marches, demonstrations and rioting with large scale arson were the norm. Not every day of course but most of it got to be routine'.[3] Within a few years of *Who Governs?*' publication, urban renewal was understood to be profoundly racialized, and observers began noting that displaced blacks were being scattered or simply left to fend for themselves in increasingly expensive urban rental markets (Schuyler 2002, Thomas 2013, Connolly 2014).

In short, with the clarity of hindsight, one can see the solidification in the 1950s – when *Who Governs?* was being researched and written – of racial gaps in northern cities that were different in kind, not just in magnitude, from the gaps among white ethnic or religious groups. As Douglas Rae puts it, 'the timing of the black migration to New Haven [in the 1950s and 1960s] was an economic horror; if the goal was to capture high-wage manufacturing jobs in and near central-city neighborhoods … the timing couldn't have been worse' (Rae 2003, p. 258). Furthermore, post-war public housing and urban renewal policies were reinforcing the older residential segregation established through municipal zoning and federal studies of 'neighborhood security'. Looking back at 1950s New Haven, Rae could point to 'the intense marginalization of black ghettos' and 'spatial hierarchy as [an] enduring institution' (Rae 2003, p. 280; see chaps. 8, 10). None of this appears in *Who Governs?*

What lessons should we draw, beyond agreeing with Yogi Berra that 'It's tough to make predictions, especially about the future'? One lesson is intellectual humility. One can never tell when a research program or publication will be overtaken by history, such that the hapless author can look foolish or shortsighted in retrospect. Colleagues of mine wrote learnedly about the long-term stability of the USSR or East Germany; other colleagues wrote about the ways in which Arab Spring would democratize the Middle East and North Africa; I wrote an essay explaining how the 2008 United States' presidential election would usher in a new policy regime of racial and economic equalization. Looking back, we can point to suggestive evidence that Dahl missed, or cognitive blinders that someone as smart as he should have been able to overcome. But if even he was unable to see a crucial failure of pluralist democracy, how much more should the rest of us avoid certitude about the issues on which we claim to be experts? (Tetlock 2005).

A second lesson is methodological, or even epistemological. One of Dahl's former students reports that the research team for *Who Governs?* debated how to make race more prominent in the analysis. After all, protests both for and against civil rights reforms were prominent in the 1950s, and 'Dahl was involved in various activities at the national level. So it seemed odd to us that race was not more salient in the New Haven study'. But given their rigorously empirical methodology, racial division appeared to play little role in the accrual and exercise of political power.

Thus, the very strength of *Who Governs?*' empirical method also turned out to be a weakness. By insisting on overt, measurable, empirical manifestations of the operation of power and influence, Dahl left out the kind of supremacy that whites held over blacks that was so strong as to be invisible in the quotidian dealings of political New Haven. This point is not new, of course; Peter Bachrach and Morton Baratz long ago asserted the importance of 'nondecisions' (Bachrach and Baratz 1962), and Steven Lukes and others have further explored the second, third, and fourth faces of power (Gaventa 1980, Isaac 1987, Lukes 2004). But it is always worth reminding ourselves that the more powerful our research method or analytic lens, the greater the risk that it leaves out something crucially important, awareness of which might profoundly change an argument.

The third lesson has an element of irony. Dahl wrote so clearly and systematically that *Who Governs?* provides most of the tools needed for its critique. The book defines crucial terms, such as influence and pluralist democracy, explains alternative patterns of leadership, instructs readers on how to study power and its uses, arrays evidence from archives to case studies to surveys and aggregated data, and articulates its broadest normative reach. A less rigorous thinker or less disciplined prose is arguably harder to criticize since the target can be obscured. The lesson for us readers is that scholarship advances more by seriously engaging with the best work of those with whom one disagrees than by picking easy marks or piling up support for one's own position.

'On Removing Certain Impediments to Democracy in the United States' offers the second, and more troubling, source of material for engaging with Dahl's inattention to racial hierarchy. It is an essay, not a major research project like *Who Governs?* Nonetheless, it shows the same great ability to organize concrete evidence in the service of large, important conclusions underlain by strong normative commitments. 'On Removing ... ' identifies five periods of consequential political decision-making in the United States' history. Before each period, 'alternative possibilities seemed open to the principal historical actors, who, however, were in conflict over the relative desirability of the alternatives they perceived'. After each period, 'what had recently been a sharply contested possibility ... came to be accepted as pretty much an undebatable aspect of the status quo' (p. 2).

The five periods are the commitment to a liberal political and constitutional order around 1800, a democratic political system by 1836, corporate capitalism by 1900, a federal welfare state in the 1930s, and involvement in the international arena as a world power in the 1940s. Without doubt these are all crucial turning points, and Dahl brilliantly lays out the choices available before each decision and their impact on American democracy, as well as their cumulative consequences for political and economic equality. But one obviously important moment is missing: the preservation of the Union and abolition of slavery in the 1860s.

Even if I were not a scholar of racial politics, the omission is startling. Surely the Civil War and the 13th, 14th, and 15th Amendments were a turning point in the eyes of any historically knowledgeable scholar; many textbooks and courses, for example, are divided into the two halves of antebellum and postbellum. But for someone as passionate about equality, democracy, and human dignity as Dahl undoubtedly was, to leave out the 1860s in a list of crucial inflection points in American history raises questions.

Dahl's writing did engage more with issues of racial hierarchy toward the end of his life, especially in *How Democratic is the American Constitution?*, published in 2003. The first of the seven ways in which the American Constitution 'fell far short of the requirements … necessary and desirable in a democratic republic' is slavery (p. 15). The second failure was the suffrage, given that it took almost 200 years for the federal government to pass an effective voting rights law. The fifth failure was equal state representation in the Senate, which 'failed to protect the fundamental rights and interests of the most deprived minorities' and gave 'some strategically placed and highly privileged minorities – slaveholders, for example – … disproportionate power'. (p. 18). Abolition of slavery was one of 'the most important amendments to the Constitution', (p. 175), just as slavery was 'the most profound violation of human rights permitted by the original constitution' (p. 27), given the 'deep wounds that slavery and its aftermath inflicted on human equality, freedom, dignity, and respect'(p. 125).

Dahl always knew how profoundly racial hierarchy violates the norms and institutions that he most cherished. But in most of his work, as 'On Removing … ' makes very clear, he focused on other dimensions of inequality, primarily economic and political. Thus, he came late to incorporating his knowledge of racial injustice into the core of his research and writing. This uncomfortable fact points to the fourth and most important lesson to emerge from considering his treatment of American racial hierarchy: the need for personal as well as intellectual humility. Dahl knew his own worth and was not falsely humble; his courtesy and kindness had a tinge of *noblesse oblige*. But he was also a genuine democrat and egalitarian, intellectually honest and willing to learn from his students. I once gathered my courage and asked why he had not included the 1860s in 'On Removing … '. He answered simply that he had been wrong and wished that he could rewrite chapters or articles, that one in particular.

If a scholar as great as Dahl continued to miss over a long period of time what now seems like a central element of his own deepest concerns, how much more vulnerable are the rest of us? I conclude that we need to be very careful about our focus on some issues to the exclusion of others, our willingness to castigate the flaws of our predecessors, our moral and empirical certitudes – lest fifty years from now some commentator points out blind spots and embarrassments in our own published record.

I learned many things from Robert Dahl; I miss him deeply.

Disclosure statement

No potential conflict of interest was reported by the author.

ROBERT A. DAHL

Notes

1. It gives me pleasure to note that I am one of only two political scientists, to my knowledge, who has been to Skagway, Alaska – population 920 in 2010 – where Dahl grew up. (The other is Stephen Wasby.) A small indicator of his personality is the fact that he went out of his way to talk with my parents, then living in Alaska, about Skagway when they visited me at Yale. Thanks to C. Anthony Broh, David Mayhew, Cynthia Verba, Sidney Verba, and an anonymous correspondent (see page xx) for helpful comments.
2. http://www.census.gov/population/www/documentation/twps0076/CTtab.pdf
3. Observation from AP photographer David Vine, at https://www.youtube.com/user/david vine

References

Bachrach, P. and Baratz, M., 1962. Two faces of power. *The American Political Science Review*, 56 (4), 947–952.

Connolly, N., 2014. *A world more concrete*. Chicago, IL: University of Chicago Press.

Dahl, R., 1957. The concept of power. *Behavioral Science*, 2 (3), 201–215.

Dahl, R., 1958. A critique of the ruling elite model. *The American Political Science Review*, 52 (2), 463–469.

Dahl, R., 1961. The behavioral approach in political science: epitaph for a monument to a successful protest. *The American Political Science Review*, 55 (4), 763–772.

Dahl, R., 1971. *Polyarchy: participation and opposition*. New Haven, CT: Yale University Press.

Dahl, R., 1977. On removing certain impediments to democracy in the United States. *Political Science Quarterly*, 92 (1), 1–20.

Dahl, R., 2003. *How democratic is the American Constitution?* 2nd ed. New Haven, CT: Yale University Press.

Dahl, R., 2005 [1961]. *Who governs? Democracy and power in an American city*. 2nd ed. New Haven, CT: Yale University Press.

Gaventa, J., 1980. *Power and powerlessness: quiescence and rebellion in an Appalachian Valley*. Urbana: University of Illinois Press.

Isaac, J., 1987. *Power and Marxist theory: a realist view*. Ithaca, NY: Cornell University Press.

Lukes, S., 2004. *Power: a radical view*. 2nd ed. London: Palgrave Macmillan.

Rae, D., 2003. *City: urbanism and its end*. New Haven, CT: Yale University Press.

Schuyler, D., 2002. *A city transformed: redevelopment, race, and suburbanization in Lancaster, Pennsylvania, 1940–1980*. University Park, PA: Pennsylvania State University Press.

Tetlock, P., 2005. *Expert political judgment: how good is it? How can we know?* Princeton, NJ: Princeton University Press.

Thomas, J., 2013. *Redevelopment and race: planning a finer city in Postwar Detroit*. Detroit, MI, Wayne State University.

Robert A. Dahl: questions, concepts, proving it

David R. Mayhew

Department of Political Science, Yale University, New Haven, USA

What were the ingredients of Robert A. Dahl's genius as a political scientist? First, he asked good questions. Those were ordinarily bold, broad questions central to political theory that appear at the openings of his works and orient them. Second, he was resourceful in creating or tailoring holistic concepts such as 'democracy' and 'power', as well as compositional categories such as 'cumulative' vs. 'noncumulative' resources, or 'participation' and 'contestation' as routes to democratization. Third, he evangelized for hypothesis testing and reliance on data-sets as the future of political science, and he acted on this advice.

Introduction

What was Robert A. Dahl's genius as a political scientist? Of the many ingredients of that genius, I would like to discuss three. They entail questions, concepts, and the use of evidence. I draw on Dahl's writings as well as, in certain details, personal acquaintance with him. I close with comments on Dahl as a democrat.

Questions

Charles E. Lindblom once asked me: 'Why does Bob Dahl stand out so much as a scholar?' I didn't know how to answer that, so I just listened. 'He asks such good questions', Lindblom said.

> That seems right. Certainly it is one feature. Dahl was upfront with the questions that animated his works. You couldn't miss them. Often they appeared in the first paragraph. They were clearly stated and obviously the product of reflection. They were broad questions that we all might want to hear an answer to, not narrow ones carrying out a theory or a method or a paradigm. Their signature content was a blend of classical political theory with the empirical complexities of the modern world. The political theory side was key. Dahl got his early training in political theory, and you couldn't read far into his works without encountering Plato, Machiavelli, Mill, Marx, Tocqueville, and the rest. Political theory was necessary as a *source* of questions for political scientists, Dahl believed. (Munck and Snyder 2007, pp. 116–119, 134, 146)

Here are some of Dahl's lead-in questions:

ROBERT A. DAHL

'What are the conditions under which numerous individuals can maximize the attainment of their goals through the use of social mechanisms?' – *Politics, Economics and Welfare*. (Dahl and Lindblom 1976, p. xlv)

Yes, this question owes to Lindblom as well as Dahl in their coauthored work first published in 1953. It is a wonderful question. It joined the processes of the economy to those of the polity. Notice the early postwar date. The authors were saying that we needed to steer past the mid-century frame of socialism vs. capitalism as a choice for organizing society. In popular discourse, a fork seemed to exist back then: choose one system or the other. Not so fast, they argued. Capitalism is a complicated, not easily graspable thing. And socialism taken as a design for effectively administering an economy, whatever else its attractions, might not work well in practice. For one thing, the British Labour Party's troubled experience in running that country's industries nationalized after World War II – Dahl and Lindblom took this record as decisive – threw cold water on the idea (Dahl and Lindblom 1976, pp. 511, 514–518). In the circumstances, analysis and aspiration needed to move elsewhere.

How does popular sovereignty function in America?' – *A Preface to Democratic Theory*.[1] (Dahl 1956)

Dahl's *Preface*, an argument drawing on political theory to sort through American experience, did much to popularize the term 'democratic theory'.

In a political system where nearly every adult may vote but where knowledge, wealth, social position, access to officials, and other resources are unequally distributed, who actually governs? – *Who Governs?* (Dahl 1961b, p. 1)

This opening sentence to *Who Governs?* may be Dahl's best-known orienting question. It grew from his experience as a federal government intern in the 1930s that showed him that political influence tends to reside in many places. It grew also from ruminations at the Center for Advanced Study in the Behavioral Sciences at Palo Alto, from living in New Haven (the focus of the study), and, finally, from research along with graduate students at Yale that came to target the 'power elite' and 'community power' ideas of C. Wright Mills and Floyd Hunter (Polsby 1980, pp. xix–xx, Dahl and Levi 2009, p. 6).

Given a regime in which the opponents of the government cannot openly and legally organize into political parties in order to oppose the government in free and fair elections, what conditions favor or impede a transformation into a regime in which they can? – *Polyarchy*. (Dahl 1971, p. 1)

This is another no-frills opening sentence. Besides Dahl's roots in political theory, this *Polyarchy* question apparently grew from his experience in Palo Alto plus a year in Rome that fed an interest in democracies beyond the US, especially the small ones. He went comparative (Munck and Snyder 2007, pp. 125–127, 140, Dahl and Levi 2009, pp. 4–5). Thus, he framed along with others the scholarly industry that keeps addressing the topic of 'democratic transitions'.

[I]s 'democracy' related in any way to 'size'? How large should a political system be in order to facilitate rational control by its citizens? – *Size and Democracy*. (Dahl and Tufte 1973, p. 1)

ROBERT A. DAHL

Coauthored with Edward R. Tufte, *Size and Democracy* combined theory with empirical analysis to address the old idea of city states and democracy. Athens was one thing, but how about today's units as diverse as the Swiss cantons, the Netherlands, the US, and India as locations of democracy?

Traction could be a problem with questions as broad as these. They called for normative or definitional judgments as well as daunting evidence. How could clipped, conclusive answers be expected? But what kinds of question should be posed at all, Dahl must have reflected. Go for the big ones. Also, by offering such questions, he aimed to show how to think about a topic freshly or to order a topic to make it more amenable to empirical investigation by others.

Concepts

Second, Dahl crafted and deployed concepts in a memorable way. Nothing is more inherent to his trademark.

By concepts I mean intellectual inventions of a certain sort – or at least tailorings of already-existent ideas – and of two different kinds. The first kind is of, let us say, holistic concepts, by which I mean characterizations devoted to some large whole area of reality – not to the parts or partitions of a reality. You cannot understand political science at its creative edges in the 1950s through the 1970s without appreciating such holistic concepts. We learned of 'modernization', 'totalitarianism', 'authoritarianism', 'civic culture', 'electoral realignments', 'political system', 'incrementalism', 'institutionalization', 'belief system', 'consociational democracy', and more. Each such term had a blended predicate of causal statements, appealing arguments of various other kinds, and well-processed facts. To organize thought in this way could have immense bite.

Enter Dahl, who became the prime deployer, or at least the sharer of that distinction, of three such holistic concepts or their families. 'Pluralism', for which it is probably fair to say that Dahl shared an updated post-World War II patent with David B. Truman, became the signature label for a kind of polity built on a jangling messiness among interests as its decision process. Yet the concept had a normative connotation too: What's wrong with that sort of politics, and who would expect anything better?[2]

A solo patent went to Dahl for his management of the term 'democracy'. This was the main thrust of his career.[3] His treatment was complicated. In 2002, Dahl looked back on defining democracy as 'an ideal type in two senses'. First, it is 'an abstract definition of what democracy would be given certain assumptions'. Second, it is 'something to be aspired to' (Munck and Snyder 2007, p. 131).[4] Neither of these two senses offers much messy reality. In tune with this ideal-typing, Dahl often supplied a list of 'criteria' that an ideal democratic process would satisfy. In one of his statements, those are: equality in voting, effective participation, enlightened understanding, final control over the agenda, and inclusion (Dahl 1982, p. 6).

But in quick order came the messy reality – the distorting shadows on the wall of the cave. With open eyes, Dahl launched 'polyarchy' as a term for what might pass as a best approximation of democracy in a large, modern, commercial state where 'politics is a sideshow in the great circus of life'.[5] Thus centered on, 'polyarchy' could be said to actually exist in a fair number of locations in the world, and Dahl wrote many works illuminating and assessing it in those locations.

ROBERT A. DAHL

Another solo patent went to Dahl for managing the terms 'power', 'influence', and sometimes 'control'.[6] This is a terminological family. As with democracy, another scholarly industry received a boost. As with democracy, we see here a characteristic methodological move. Dahl called on terms with long histories of often discordant popular usage and brisked them up for deployment in the social sciences. They took on new precision as analytic tools. Thus marshaled, they could solve some questions, open up others, and sometimes bring on fierce new controversies. der Muhll (1977), p. 1080) has summed up Dahl's definition of 'power' or 'influence' as 'a demonstrably asymmetrical causal connection among actors'. There could be wrinkles. Influence, for example, could be 'indirect' as opposed to 'direct', or 'potential' as opposed to 'actual' (Dahl 1961b, css. 12, 24).

Beyond these holistic concepts, Dahl also organized his work in a series of what might be called compositional concepts. By this, I mean sets of subsidiary concepts that contribute to some whole. This was a much-repeated intellectual strategy. Two principles seem to have been in play. On the one hand, Dahl's instinct was to decompose, to be literally analytic (der Muhll 1977, p. 1094). Often, he showed by example, a good way to understand a topic is to break it into pieces in a fashion that assigns a credible essence to each piece and then examine the pieces and the relations among them. On the other hand, his instinct was to simplify. Science means simplification. 'Without simplification you cannot deal with complexity. You need some kind of map that simplifies reality', Dahl once remarked (Munck and Snyder 2007, p. 136). And an especially fine comment:

> It's like looking out at the stars at night. It's great to look out at night and see the stars but you're not understanding anything about the nature of the universe. It has to be simplified. And in simplification you lose some potential information, but the gain is to provide comprehensibility and coherence. (Dahl and Levi 2009, p. 7)

Decompose, the advice of these seemingly competing mandates is, but not into too many pieces. The pieces need to be simplifications themselves, and the array of them needs to be small in number and readily graspable.

This brand of organizing scheme appears in many of Dahl's works. Following are several instances.

Politics, Economics and Welfare (with Lindblom) centers on 'four central sociopolitical processes' that '[a]ll modern industrialized economies combine, though in different ways' (Dahl and Lindblom 1976, p. 369). Where did the authors get this quartet of processes? Well, they created it. Analytically, it was a way to proceed. There is 'the price system', the territory of competitive markets. There is 'hierarchy', by which the authors meant control by bureaucratic leaders in both the governmental and private organizations of modern societies. There is 'polyarchy', or control of leaders by publics – a taste in 1953 of Dahl's concept that would keep appearing. And there is 'bargaining', a form of 'reciprocal control among leaders' – an idea that the authors applied especially to interactions within government.[7] One suspects that Dahl drew on his experience working for the federal government in the late 1930s and World War II for devising the second and fourth of these categories – the hierarchy and bargaining. He worked in the National Labor Relations Board, the Department of Agriculture, the Office of Price Administration, and the War Production Board, not to mention the US Army (Munck and Snyder 2007, p. 115, Dahl and Levi 2009, p. 1). (He told me once

ROBERT A. DAHL

about marching into Austria in 1945.) This surprising richness of experience – how many academics could match it? – had to be an education in the disorderliness of government processes American-style. At any rate, socialism vs. capitalism, Dahl and Lindblom were saying as of 1953, was an unpromising frame for seeing the real or likely processes of society. Better their four ideas than this popular dualism.

Dahl's categories in *A Preface to Democratic Theory* are meant to be illustrative rather than exhaustive: 'I shall take up a few representative types of democratic theory, beginning with one that is familiar to Americans' (Dahl 1956, p. 2). That number one is 'Madisonian Democracy' – a formally guaranteed compromise between the power of majorities and the power of minorities. Next comes 'Populist Democracy', which he handles as a purely abstract principle of majority rule that can raise questions of intensity, interpersonal comparison of utilities, the Arrow Problem, and so on. These first two categories are 'maximizing' theories. But then he moves to his satisficing number three, yes, 'Polyarchal Democracy'.[8] This category is strongly empirical. It embraces the disorderly, imperfect, fallback reality of how American democracy has actually worked. In *A Preface*, the fallback version doesn't look all that bad. At its core, the book is an interplay among these three categories. Number three wins out. In Dahl's well-known account, formal Madisonianism suffers the difficulty of not accounting for democracy well. Britain, Sweden, and other countries do not need formal separation of powers in their national institutions to make democracy work, so why should the US? Q.E.D. Populist Democracy, for all its smartness, suffers the difficulty of not hitting the ground. Hence an analytic retreat to real American experience, where, among other things, it is often true as a matter of informal practice that 'minorities rule' (Dahl 1956, p. 128). Overarching it all, the country's unceasing election processes at least help insure 'that political leaders will be somewhat responsive to the preferences of some ordinary citizens' (Dahl 1956, p. 131).

At the core of *Who Governs?* are five compositional concepts. In analytic terms, what were the possible patterns of influence in the city of New Haven in the 1950s (Dahl 1961b, chs. 15–18)? The first, 'Covert integration by Economic Notables', proved on investigation to be a blank. Dahl, his eye on community power theory, took obvious delight in torpedoing the hypothesis of an 'essentially clandestine or covert exercise of influence by the 'real' leaders' of the city, perhaps operating by 'covert negotiations and discussions carried on in the privacy of their clubs, homes, business firms, and other private meeting places'. An industrious hunt by Dahl and his research team brought no evidence of such a cabal.[9] Category number two, 'An executive-centered "grand coalition of coalitions"', hit some pay dirt (Dahl 1961b, p. 184). It accommodated the large, ad hoc coalition that Mayor Richard C. Lee assembled in the public spotlight to pursue urban redevelopment in the 1950s (Dahl 1961b, ch. 17). Dahl does not do much to develop his category three, 'A coalition of chieftains'.[10] Category four, 'Independent sovereignties with spheres of influence' (Dahl 1961b, p. 199), could accommodate 'the various petty sovereignties that made up the official and unofficial government of New Haven'. A neighborhood controversy over building metal houses supplied an instance (Dahl 1961b, ch. 16, quotation at p. 190). Category five, 'Rival sovereignties fighting it out', could apply to ordinary competition between the city's two political parties. The Republicans were still a force in the 1950s (Dahl 1961b, ch. 18). This quintet of categories, a product of crossing theory with evidence, seemed to fit the reality.

ROBERT A. DAHL

Separately, an analytic dualism infuses *Who Governs?* A society's inequalities in politically relevant resources – wealth, social standing, sources of information, the vote, control over jobs, and so on – may be 'cumulative' or they may be 'non-cumulative' – a synonym for 'dispersed' (Dahl 1961b, chs. 1, 7). The history of New Haven, in Dahl's telling, had progressed from the former condition to the latter (Dahl 1961b, Book I). In the late eighteenth century, a Puritan oligarchy enjoyed a lock on all relevant resources. By the mid-twentieth century, supplies of resources were scattered across social classes, ethnic groups, professional specialists, and elsewhere. Pluralism had arrived. Various kinds of actors could maneuver and prevail on various kinds of matters (Dahl 1961b, Books IV, V).

One line of analytic enterprise is to decompose time into eras – as in the 'electoral realignment eras' proposed by various authors in the 1960s. So far as I can tell, Dahl showed no interest in the realignments research program, and, in general, the ordering of time was not his game. But the eras motif does make an appearance in *Who Governs?*, and there is another interesting instance. In a 1977 piece, Dahl sorted the two centuries of American experience into five 'historical commitments' that he saw the country having arrived at. In each case, bitter conflict gave way to, if not consensus, at least lasting acceptance on a fundamental matter. These commitments were to: a constitutional and liberal order in the late eighteenth century, democracy in the nineteenth century, corporate capitalism starting in the 1890s, a welfare state in the 1930s, and an international role as a world power in the 1940s (Dahl 1977, pp. 2–4). We see here the concept of a 'historical commitment' as well as a workout of it in manageable specifics.

In the 1960s, Dahl (1966) edited a project that ended in essays on 'political oppositions' in 10 Western democracies. What to make of it all? That was a teaser. The essays as well as the countries they reported on were a heterogeneous lot. Dahl decided to focus on the important ways that oppositions can differ. He came up with six ways: an opposition's cohesion, its competitiveness, its site of opposing the government, its distinctiveness, its goals, and its strategies (ch. 11). Italy with its Communist Party, Belgium with its communal division, Britain with its 'loyal opposition', and the US with its diffuse and confusing processes were among the countries that needed to be accommodated in these cells. Political opposition in democracies is a complicated matter.

Finally, there is the compositional scheme in *Polyarchy*. Little in the Dahl canon has enjoyed more resonance. In especially European history, he saw the evolution toward democracy as having two dimensions. One was toward the 'participation' (or 'inclusion') of publics. The other was toward effective 'contestation' in politics (or 'liberalization') (Dahl 1971, ch. 1). Conceptually, to pair each of these achievements with its absence allowed that favorite device of social scientists – a fourfold table (Dahl 1971, p. 7). From such a design, Dahl guided a comparative history. Contestation in advance of participation could be good news for eventual democracy as in the cases of Britain and Sweden. The reverse could be bad news as in Germany's Second Reich. Simultaneous moves to participation and contestation could bring big trouble as in France in the 1790s. The trick was favorable sequencing (Dahl 1971, ch. 3).

Concepts, categories, classifications: What kind of activity is it to develop ideas like these? Art as well as science seems to figure. The terms need to be grounded in reality, and the right joints need to be cut at, but there is no getting around having an inspired intuition and flexing it in an appealing way.

ROBERT A. DAHL

Proving it

What was the behavioral revolution in American political science in the postwar years? According to Dahl (1961a, p. 766), widely seen as its signature leader, it was 'a protest movement' against the 'historical, philosophical, and the descriptive–institutional approaches' that had long marked the discipline. Political science at that time, possessed of a feisty new generation of scholars short on patience, needed a reset. To find out what was actually true or not – that was the way to go. It meant becoming more scientific.

For Dahl, that meant for one thing an attraction to the ideas of Carl Hempel, the philosopher of science then at Yale, an exponent of positivism (Munck and Snyder 2007, p. 122). It meant a search for 'genuinely testable propositions' (Dahl and Lindblom 1976, p. xlv). Dahl became an evangelist for the idea of hypothesis testing. That was the sort of thing political scientists should be doing. A commonplace idea now, it was not commonplace going into the 1950s. To read into *A Preface* or *Polyarchy* is to encounter blizzards of suggestions for hypotheses that might be tested. Axioms, assumptions, definitions, conditions, and propositions, not to mention logical symbols, make an appearance. It is a style of argument.[11] James Madison wouldn't have known what hit him:

> There ensues [in *The Federalist*] an extremely dubious and probably false set of propositions … (Dahl 1956, p. 16)

But how should hypotheses actually be tested? In much of his work, Dahl pursued abstract theory of one type or another, but he was formidable in full fledge as an empirical researcher. He did field work, as for his first book *Congress and Foreign Policy* in 1950. 'I figured if I was going to write about Congress, I needed to know about it, and that required talking to some people. I did a lot of interviews, and that was quite enlightening' (Munck and Snyder 2007, p. 139). This is another practice that seems commonplace now but was not that going into the 1950s – certainly not in congressional studies, where arm's-length scholarship had been standard.

Who Governs? is Dahl's masterpiece of empirical work. He designed it as a multi-method enterprise. There was field work. He and his graduate assistants Nelson W. Polsby and Raymond Wolfinger conducted 46 lengthy interviews with participants in significant New Haven decisions. Wolfinger interned in the city government. (Both Polsby and Wolfinger got dissertations out of the project.) Dahl supervised three sample surveys. He had students in a seminar prepare detailed events studies. He used aggregate voting data. He drew on various historical materials, including standard histories, the US Census, city directories, and other documents and records.[12] The Dahl research team zeroed in on New Haven in these complementary ways.

In empirical terms, perhaps the leading theme in Dahl's work is: Get hold of a data-set and use it. That is what you need to do if you want to figure out if something is true or not. If possible, count things. (I remember V. O. Key, Jr. also proselytizing for this view in the 1950s.) Again, this piece of advice is standard in political science today but it hasn't always been. Often Dahl crafted his own data-sets, sometimes he drew on other people's. In all cases, it is probably fair to say, the questions he wanted to tackle preceded his data-sets rather than vice versa. At base, he was question-driven, not data-set-driven.

ROBERT A. DAHL

To appreciate Dahl, it helps to get a sense of his data-sets and their use. Below is a sample. I include instances where he cites an N and performs arithmetic with it, but also instances where he somehow canvassed, with seeming credibility, a full universe of something and arrived at a judgment about it without reporting the N or the arithmetic. The key to it all is a mindset of stipulating a universe and then examining the items in it.

- Of the 57 successful actions [regarding urban redevelopment in New Haven], half can be attributed to only two persons: the Mayor and the Development Administrator. (Dahl 1961b, p. 124)
- [O]f the 29 countries with polyarchal regimes in 1970, in only 12 was polyarchy inaugurated after independence and not during a period of overt foreign domination. (Dahl 1971, p. 197)
- Yet in the 120 years since the Communist Manifesto was published, no country has developed according to the Marxist model of conflict, nor has any regime, whether hegemonic or competitive, fallen or been transformed because of a clear-cut polarization of working-class and bourgeoisie. (Dahl 1971, p. 106)
- Specifically, there seems to be no significant relationship between turnout in national elections and population, area, or density among some 33 representative democracies. (Dahl and Tufte 1973, p. 44).
- Madison proved to be right [this time]. There has, in fact, never been a significant conflict between the citizens of small states and the citizens of large states. (Dahl 1967, p. 52).
- Over its whole history, the Supreme Court has held Congressional legislation unconstitutional in 77 cases … [Yet] [t]here is, I believe, no case on record where a persistent law-making majority [that is, a succession of elected officials] has not, sooner or later, achieved its purposes. (Dahl 1956, pp. 109–110)
- [N]ot one of the 50 prominent citizens interviewed in the course of this study – citizens who had participated extensively in various decisions – hinted at the existence of such a cabal [that is, an elite of Economic Notables operating covertly in New Haven]. (Dahl 1961b, p. 185)

Dahl mastered and discussed the intricacies of his data-sets. That was necessary to their use. The wrinkles could be as informative as the regularities. In his New Haven study, the neighborhood uprising against building metal houses showed that the "slack' resources' of the system could, given the right provocation, turn un-slack in a hurry (Dahl 1961b, pp. 192–199, quotation at p. 305). In the prose or footnotes of *Polyarchy*, he discusses by my count 58 individual countries for one reason or another and hits another 14 in the accompanying charts.[13] Deviant cases drew his curiosity – Argentina for its underperformance, the Netherlands for its ethic of accommodation, India for a variety of reasons including size (Dahl 1971, pp. 135–140, 160–161, 204–205).

The behavioral revolution came in the 1950s and 1960s. Years later, Dahl was not all that enthusiastic about another dose of science – the rational choice revolution. His view: 'As important as rational choice theory may be in dealing with some types of problems, it's not a satisfactory way of dealing with the most important problems' (Munck and Snyder 2007, pp. 124, 147, quotation at p. 147). 'It cannot encompass the empirical variety and complexity of the world' (Dahl and

ROBERT A. DAHL

Levi 2009, p. 8). Also, I would guess that he wasn't willing to give up on classical political theory as a source of orienting questions, and that by his nature, he was too much of an inductivist to buy into rational choice.

Dahl the democrat

Dahl's work was a blend of the normative and the positive. I have emphasized the positive side. His questions and concepts faced both ways, yet they ordinarily fed somehow into empirics – certainly in his quest for hypothesis testing.

But I would like to close by taking a look at Dahl as a democrat – both small-D and in American terms capital-D, although on the latter front, Dahl wasn't a very aggressive partisan. Generally speaking, he sort of went along with partisanship American-style, rather than getting obsessed by it. He was a cool partisan.

Where did Dahl's small-D democracy come from and what did it consist of? He left some nice testimony on these points. There is a frontier flavor. Growing up chiefly in the Alaska panhandle (Iowa figured previously, too), a coastal site of primary sector industry, seems to have left a mark. He wrote a fond book about the experience late in his life (2005). From a doctor's family, Dahl earned money working on the docks with longshoremen starting at age 12, where, in his words, 'I came into contact with of course the local people I already knew, but also on the docks, people whom I didn't know, working people, and that exposed me to an aspect of life which I've never forgotten'. That experience, as well as 'my military service, and growing up in a small town, just gave me a very deep and lasting respect for – what is often said, 'ordinary people.' I don't like that term. But just plain ordinary human beings. I respect them for, among other things, they've got degrees of common sense which are not always so obviously present in our colleagues and other intellectuals' (Dahl and Levi 2009, pp. 2–3).

Yes, there was the challenge of education: People needed to be informed in order to protect their interests – a recurrent Dahl theme.[14] But generally speaking, the 'common sense' of the public deserves respect. Beware of intellectuals or anyone else trying to tell ordinary people what or how they should think. Dahl keeps coming back to this point. 'Who is a better judge than I of what my "will," my policy, really is?' (Dahl 1967, p. 17).

> In making governmental decisions, among adults no person or group is better qualified, with only extremely rare exceptions, to judge what those interests are and thus to substitute their judgment for that of the person whose interests are affected. The claim of one group to possess superior knowledge of the interests of another group of persons, and also to possess a reliable commitment to protect those interests, seems to me utterly falsified by historical experience. (Munck and Snyder 2007, p. 130)

It is easy to slide over statements like these. They seem like bromides. But read them carefully. Dahl crafted them with care, and they seem to have expressed a bedrock ingredient of small-D democracy as well as a moral imperative.[15] He meant that victory in policy-making should ordinarily go to the views of ordinary people – arrived at by themselves – not to the didacticisms of liberals, progressives, conservatives, prophets, private corporations, unions, judges, the media, or whatever. Among the American chattering classes of today, this is a surprisingly rare stance.

How did Dahl's belief in small-D democracy play into his personal positioning in the partisan and ideological politics of the US? The following is speculation. For

ROBERT A. DAHL

the first half of the twentieth century into the 1950s, the side of American politics inhabited by progressives, liberals, and Democrats seized on majority rule as one of its emphatic premises and aims.[16] The thinking is familiar. Fundamentally, politics was seen to hinge on social class at least in the home-grown American sense of the people vs. the special interests. Given this stipulated map of interests and preferences, a successful execution of majority rule meant that ordinary people in a class sense would beat the special interests. The role of the progressives and the rest was to steer politics through a customary clutter of institutional, moneyed, and private organizational obstacles to achieve this agreeable end. Key to it all was the principle of majority rule.

Again, Dahl was not a ferocious partisan, but his range of writing insofar as it bleeds partisanship or ideology seems to locate him as above. The driving political views of ordinary people are economic; majority rule allows those views to prevail; that is a good thing; generally speaking, the progressive side helps along that end-state so two cheers for it. One clear clue to Dahl's personal positioning is his affection for the New Deal. He came of age with it. It 'influenced my conviction that change is possible' and left a lasting positive impression (Munck and Snyder 2007, p. 138). To be sure, majority rule for Dahl was not a clipped, arithmetic thing. In the American tradition, it sported curlicues of intensity expression, slack resources, cross-cutting cleavages, 'minorities rule', and the rest, but at the end of the day it was, or should be, the process to which everyone would have to accommodate, and it was a framework favorable to ordinary people. It was favorable in that way in the 1930s.

Dahl was a New Deal-ish liberal, not a socialist – at least not after an early-years fling with Norman Thomas socialism (Dahl and Levi 2009, p. 2). Then he wrote his Yale dissertation about socialism – Ph.D. 1940 – and gave it up (Munck and Snyder 2007, pp. 119–120). He was never a Marxist. The analytic moves of Marxism left him cold (Munck and Snyder 2007, pp. 117, 119). Later in his life, when the American and European center-lefts were growing hard to tell apart, he still wasn't 'terribly comfortable' being characterized as a democratic socialist –

> in part because I discovered when I was in graduate school doing my dissertation the deep dark secret of socialists (and I thought of myself as a socialist at the time): They really had no realistic conception of how to operate an economic order, or for that matter, a democratic political system. (Cameron *et al.* 1988, p. 159)

But a basic economistic ontology of politics – that it is about economic stratification – as well as a frame for accommodating that ontology – majority rule – seems to have stayed with Dahl. Those were basics. Beginning in the 1960s, the American left drifted into race and multiculturalism as an alternative ontology of cleavage. Dahl didn't do that. Certainly he deplored the historical American racial order, and he wrote about it (1961b, pp. 293–296, 1967, pp. 65–67). He had an apt phrase for the traditional South – 'a kind of polyarchy for whites and hegemony for blacks' (1971, p. 28). He was a strong civil rights advocate. But race was never central to his writing. Also, as the American left came to rely on the judiciary to pursue its rights causes, thus ceding populist ground to a Republican Party engaging the white working-class – who was the champion of majority rule anymore? – Dahl stayed put. In general, in the long run, rights could be protected best by the ordinary swordplay of competitive politics. Rule by judges, after all, is not an expression of democracy.[17]

ROBERT A. DAHL

How well was democracy working in the US? On this question, Dahl did drift somewhat. He was pretty happy about things in the fifties and sixties. The New Deal had set a pleasing course, and compared with what? Before, during, or after World War II, who could avoid watching or remembering the horrors elsewhere in the world? (Munck and Snyder 2007, p. 138). Although not lacking problems, the American system was not 'so obviously a defective system as some of its critics suggest' (Dahl 1956, p. 150). In democratic terms, it was one of a small pack of the world's success stories (Dahl 1956, p. 74).

> [I]t appears to be a relatively efficient system for reinforcing agreement, encouraging moderation, and maintaining social peace in a restless and immoderate people operating a gigantic, powerful, diversified, and incredibly complex society. (Dahl 1956, p. 151)[18]

The jangling pluralism of New Haven came off well in *Who Governs?* The country's 'democratic creed' was available as a backup crutch in the face of, say, McCarthyism (Dahl 1961b, ch. 28).

But after the 1960s, Dahl soured somewhat on the American record. One sees this in a fresh preface to *Politics, Economics and Welfare* in 1976 (although on rereading this preface, I guessed that it owed an awful lot to coauthor Lindblom). Concerned about business power, Dahl came to write about the 'corporate leviathan' and the potential of worker control within firms (Dahl 1970, pp. 115–140). He grew especially worried about 'the extent of economic inequality among Americans'. Perhaps a pluralistic system of the American kind, for all its virtues, was a dubious bet to lessen that inequality (Dahl 1978, pp. 199–201). Once one of the democratic pack, the US was sliding into downside outlier status. There were better models elsewhere. This country was 'a long way from having achieved the redistributive policies of the Scandinavian countries' (Dahl 1982, p. 119). And not just the Scandinavians (Dahl 1982, p. 174–175).

A theorist of democracy needs to wrestle with the American Constitution, and Dahl repeatedly did that. He was not a fan of the Constitution. In his early writing, he saw it as gratuitous but largely harmless. It was an eighteenth-century settlement that unfortunately butted into a nineteenth-century polity that was naturally crystallizing into a Tocquevillian ideal-type of democracy and that reached that destination anyway. The separation-of-powers design of the Constitution was not much of an impediment. As a practical matter, Thomas Jefferson's spirit of popular control proved a fair match for Madison's complicating blueprints.[19]

But the Constitution gnawed at Dahl. He really didn't like it. It was not that he bought into the standard Beardian interpretation that a crafty upper-class self-servingly wrote it (Dahl 1967, pp. 32–34). He just didn't like the provisions. Thus witness his recent 2002 book, *How Democratic Is the American Constitution?*, which opened with a blockbuster of an orienting question that left no doubt about the content to follow:

> Why should we feel bound today by a document produced more than two centuries ago by a group of fifty-five mortal men, actually signed by only thirty-nine, a fair number of whom were slaveholders, and adopted in only thirteen states by the votes of fewer than two thousand men, all of whom are long since dead and mainly forgotten? (Dahl 2002, p. 2)

ROBERT A. DAHL

In this work, he offered chiefly a formalist critique of the Constitution – the crazy electoral college, the Wyoming to California makeup of the Senate, judicial review, and certain other features that in early days, impeded rule by national majorities – slavery, no popular election of senators, state control of the suffrage, and weak congressional taxing and regulatory powers. National majorities of the public were and are procedurally hamstrung, or they can be. That was his spirited treatment (ch. 2). He went on to a case about consequences: the American system doesn't work any better than a peer group of countries in maintaining democratic stability, protecting rights, ensuring fairness, encouraging consensus, or solving problems. Yet, those other countries get along without Madisonian constitutions (ch. 5). Case made. This is the kind of argument Dahl once offered in *Polyarchy*. Surprisingly, at least in light of current public dialog, there is nothing in the *Constitution* book suggesting a causal path between the operations of the Constitution and the country's condition of relative economic inequality. Dahl steered clear of that one. He was always a careful, evidence-based arguer.

Disclosure statement

No potential conflict of interest was reported by the author.

Notes

1. The question cited here appears on the cover of the book as a kind of subtitle, although it is not exactly that.
2. 'Pluralism' as term and idea wends its way through Dahl's work, notably in *Who Governs?* (1961b), *Pluralist Democracy in the United States* (1967), Pluralism Revisited (1978), and *Dilemmas of Pluralist Democracy* (1982).
3. Culminating in *Democracy and Its Critics* (1989).
4. The year of this book's interview with Dahl was 2002.
5. Dahl discusses drawing on the term 'polyarchy' in Dahl and Levi (2009, p. 5). The sideshow quotation is from Dahl (1961b, p. 305).
6. As in Dahl (1957, 1982, ch. 2), Dahl and Stinebrickner (2003, ch. 2).
7. The authors deploy these four categories in respectively chs. 6–13 of Dahl and Lindblom (1976). The phrase 'reciprocal control among leaders,' which Dahl also uses in later work, appears at p. 324.
8. These three theories are taken up in respectively chs. 1–3 of Dahl (1956).
9. This theory is pursued in ch. 6 and also at pp. 184–186 of Dahl (1961b), quotation at p. 184.
10. Dahl (1961b, pp. 186–187) left open the possibility that the idea might apply better in other settings such as Congress.
11. As seen in Dahl (1956, chs. 1, 2, 1971, ch. 1).
12. Discussions of the enterprise appear in Dahl (1961b, p. vi and Appendix B), and in Munck and Snyder (2007, p. 139).
13. There are more yet in the book's appendixes.
14. It makes an appearance directly after the quoted material of the previous paragraph.
15. On the idea as moral imperative: Munck and Snyder (2007, p. 130).
16. See the argument in Gerring (2001, ch. 6).
17. Dahl's suspicion of judicial review went way back, but it was still lively, if not un-asterisked, in Dahl's (2002) *How Democratic Is the American Constitution?*, pp. 152–154.
18. A similar summary judgment appears in Dahl's (1967, p. 4) American politics text.
19. These judgments about the history come across in Dahl (1967, chs. 2, 3).

ROBERT A. DAHL

References

Cameron, D.R., et al., 1988. Roundtable discussion: politics, economics, and welfare. *In*: I. Shapiro and G. Reeher, eds. *Power, inequality, and democratic politics: essays in honor of Robert A. Dahl*. Boulder, CO: Westview, 153–167.

Dahl, R.A., 1950. *Congress and Foreign Policy*. New York, NY: W.W. Norton.

Dahl, R.A., 1956. *A preface to democratic theory*. Chicago, IL: The University of Chicago Press.

Dahl, R.A., 1957. The concept of power. *Behavioral Science*, 2 (3), 201–215.

Dahl, R.A., 1961a. The behavioral approach in political science: epitaph for a monument to a successful protest. *The American Political Science Review*, 55 (4), 763–772.

Dahl, R.A., 1961b. *Who governs? Democracy and power in an American city*. New Haven, CT: Yale University Press.

Dahl, R.A., ed., 1966. *Political oppositions in western democracies*. New Haven, CT: Yale University Press.

Dahl, R.A., 1967. *Pluralist democracy in the United States: conflict and consent*. Chicago, IL: Rand McNally.

Dahl, R.A., 1970. *After the revolution? Authority in a good society*. New Haven, CT: Yale University Press.

Dahl, R.A., 1971. *Polyarchy: participation and opposition*. New Haven, CT: Yale University Press.

Dahl, R.A., 1977. On removing certain impediments to democracy in the United States. *Political Science Quarterly*, 92 (1), 1–20.

Dahl, R.A., 1978. Pluralism revisited. *Comparative Politics*, 10 (2), 191–203.

Dahl, R.A., 1982. *Dilemmas of pluralist democracy: autonomy vs. control*. New Haven, CT: Yale University Press.

Dahl, R.A., 1989. *Democracy and its critics*. New Haven, CT: Yale University Press.

Dahl, R.A., 2002. *How democratic is the American constitution?* New Haven, CT: Yale University Press.

Dahl, R.A., 2005. *After the gold rush: growing up in Skagway*. Bloomington, IN: Xlibris.

Dahl, R.A. and Levi, M., 2009. A conversation with Robert A. Dahl. *Annual Review of Political Science*, 12, 1–9.

Dahl, R.A. and Lindblom, C.E., 1976. *Politics, economics and welfare: planning and politico-economic systems resolved into basic social processes*. 2nd ed. Chicago, IL: The University of Chicago Press.

Dahl, R.A. and Stinebrickner, B., 2003. *Modern political analysis*. 6th ed. Upper Saddle River, NJ: Prentice Hall.

Dahl, R.A. and Tufte, E.R., 1973. *Size and democracy*. Stanford University Press.

Gerring, J., 2001. *Party ideologies in the America, 1828–1996*. Stanford, CA: Cambridge University Press.

der Muhll, G., 1977. Robert A. Dahl and the study of contemporary democracy: a review essay. *The American Political Science Review*, 71 (3), 1070–1096.

Munck, G.L. and Snyder, R., eds., 2007. *Passion, craft, and method in comparative politics*. Baltimore, MD: The Johns Hopkins University Press.

Polsby, N.W., 1980. *Community power & political theory: a further look at problems of evidence and inference*. New Haven, CT: Yale University Press.

Robert A. Dahl and the essentials of *Modern Political Analysis*: politics, influence, power, and polyarchy

Bruce Stinebrickner

Department of Political Science, DePauw University, Greencastle, IN, USA

In *Modern Political Analysis* (*MPA*), Robert A. Dahl presents what he saw as the essentials of politics and political science. Spanning four decades of Dahl's scholarly career, the six editions of *MPA* address (i) the nature of politics; (ii) 'influence', the constituent element of politics and *MPA*'s term for what political scientists often call 'power'; and (iii) similarities and differences among political systems. Seven 'forms of influence' – power, coercion, force, persuasion, manipulation, inducement, and authority – are distinguished and analyzed. In exploring similarities and differences among the world's political systems, *MPA* presents an overview of Dahl's insights on democracy and polyarchy. The six *MPA* editions also provide an opportunity to observe how Dahl's thinking about the essentials of his discipline evolved over forty years.

The first edition of Robert A. Dahl's *Modern Political Analysis* (hereafter *MPA*) appeared in 1963 and the last edition in 2003. Ranging from 118 (1st edition) to 172 pages (6th edition) and intended primarily as a short text for undergraduate and postgraduate students, the six editions of *MPA* address what Dahl, arguably the most renowned political scientist of his era, saw as the essentials of his discipline. The books also reflect the evolution of his thinking about those essentials over four decades.

The first edition of *MPA* was the inaugural book and flagship of what publisher Prentice-Hall called its *Foundations of Modern Political Science Series*, for which Dahl served as general editor. In 1970, the second edition of *MPA* listed nineteen books in the series, and the total of projected volumes had risen to twenty-one by the appearance of the fourth edition of *MPA* in 1984. The list of authors of these slim volumes – typically running to no more than about 150 pages – reads like a partial *Who's Who* of American political scientists in the 1960s and 1970s, with a heavy concentration of Dahl's colleagues, former colleagues, or former graduate students from Yale's illustrious department of that era. Included among 'Foundations' authors were Karl Deutsch (*The Analysis of International Relations*), Charles E. Lindblom (*The Policy Making Process*), Robert E. Lane and David O. Sears (*Public Opinion*), Edward R. Tufte (*Data Analysis in Political Science*), Nelson W. Polsby (*Congress and the Presidency*), and Fred I. Greenstein (*The American Party System and the American People*).

ROBERT A. DAHL

In a passage appearing in the prefaces in each of the first four *MPA* editions, Dahl writes that

> this book does not pretend to tell you all that you need to know about politics. Its aim is more modest but more realistic: to equip you with a small number of basic concepts, ideas, and analytical tools – ancient or recent, whichever seem the better – so that you proceed afterward with more competence toward what should be, in a democracy, a life-long vocation: the analysis of politics. (1963, p. viii)

In his preface to *MPA* 2nd, Dahl sounds a theme echoed in subsequent *MPA* prefaces and reflected in all succeeding editions of MPA:

> I have found it necessary to change more than I had intended when I embarked on the task [of revision]. Changes have been required not only because my own ideas have been altered on some matters … but also – and this is the major cause of change – because so much new and directly relevant material has appeared in the brief period since I finished the manuscript for the first edition. The need to revise this volume is testimony, I think, to the vigor of modern political science. (1970, p. vi)[1]

All six *MPA* editions embrace fundamental points that Dahl held throughout his celebrated career: that there is a great deal to know and investigate about politics and that neither a single book nor a single political scientist can do it all; that basic concepts, ideas, and analytical tools are essential means to understanding politics; that both classical writings and modern political science have much to contribute; and that democratic theory and the contemporary practice of democracy are centrally important objects of political analysis.

Three major foci anchor all six *MPA* editions during four decades of evolution:

(1) the nature of politics (every *MPA* edition contains a chapter entitled 'What Is Politics?');
(2) conceptual distinctions among influence, power, persuasion, authority, coercion, and related phenomena, and the roles of these phenomena in political systems; and
(3) differences and similarities among political systems, particularly national political systems, with special attention to contemporary democracies.

In pursuing the third focus, the *MPA* books provide an instructive overview of many foundational elements in Dahl's corpus of works on democracy and democratic theory. The six editions – especially but not only in their prefaces – also convey the author's thinking about some noteworthy developments in the discipline of political science over the last four decades of the twentieth century. All this makes reading (or rereading) and reflecting on *MPA* worthwhile – both as a manual on how to approach and do political analysis and an overview of modern political science as seen by one of its most accomplished practitioners.

This article will proceed by treating each of the three major foci in *MPA* in turn. It will conclude by addressing how the three foci cohere with one another to create a composite picture of Dahl's conception of politics, democracy, and how political analysis ought to proceed.

ROBERT A. DAHL

The nature of politics

Appearing in all six *MPA* editions is a Venn diagram that is given the title 'Definitions of Politics' in the last three editions (1963, p. 6). Accompanying the diagram in the text is a comparison of Aristotle's, Max Weber's, and Harold Lasswell's partly overlapping and partly diverging perspectives about what constitutes politics. 'Aristotle, Weber, and Lasswell, and almost all other political scientists, agree that political relationships are to be found somewhere within … the set of relationships involving power, rule, or authority' (1963, p. 5). For Lasswell, according to *MPA*, that is the beginning and the end of the story: 'political science … [is] "the study of the shaping and sharing of power"' (1963, p. 5). In contrast, 'Aristotle and Weber … define the term "political" so as to require one or more additional characteristics' (1963, p. 5). For Weber, 'the domain of the political' involves *both* power, rule, or authority *and* territoriality. For the 'less clear' Aristotle, 'the domain of the political' is, according to *MPA*, limited to 'relationships in associations capable of self-sufficiency' (1963, p. 5).

Ultimately, MPA declares that 'politics is simply *the exercise of influence*' (2003, p. 24, emphasis in original).[2] Though *MPA* asserts that this definition is 'in the tradition of Lasswell and countless other contemporary political scientists' (2003, p. 24), the title and contents of Lasswell's *Politics: Who Gets What, When, How* (1936) suggest otherwise. For Lasswell, politics does indeed center on influence and power, and the first chapter of *Politics: Who Gets What, When, How* begins with 'The study of politics is the study of influence and the influential' (p. 3). Lasswellian politics, however, also involves political actors 'striv[ing] … for the attainment of various values for which power is a necessary (and perhaps also sufficient) condition' (Lasswell and Kaplan 1950, p. 240). While Lasswell sees politics as the exercise of power or influence in efforts to obtain valued outcomes, *MPA*'s conception of politics centers entirely on influence.

While this Dahl–Lasswell difference might be seen as splitting conceptual or definitional hairs, Dahl's influence-centric notion of politics, which anchors all six *MPA* editions, can be put into sharper perspective by raising a well-known conception of politics prominently advanced in the 1950s by fellow political scientist David Easton: 'the authoritative allocation of values for a society' (1953, p. 129, 1965a, pp. 47–57). During the 1960s, Dahl's power/influence orientation and Easton's 'authoritative allocation of values for a society' were seen by some as competitors with one another. Confusing who said what in this definitional rivalry, *The New York Times* obituary marking Dahl's death in February 2014 (Martin 2014) erroneously attributed Easton's definition of 'politics' to Dahl, which evoked cries of disbelief among some political scientists, including me.

The wording '*seen* as … competitors with one another [emphasis added]' in the preceding paragraph is intentional, for a careful reading of relevant passages by Easton appears to close, but not eliminate, the gap between him and Dahl on what politics is. In *The Political System,* Easton writes that 'neither the concept of the state *nor that of power* is satisfactory even as a rough approximation' [of] 'political life' (1953, p. 126, emphasis added). Twenty pages later he observes that a definition of politics focusing on power

> is a truncated and at the same time overambitious interpretation of the central political variable. The very most that we could say is that there is a close tie between the pattern of values stemming from any authoritative allocation and the distribution and use

ROBERT A. DAHL

of power. Political science is the study of the authoritative allocation *as it is influenced by the distribution and use of power.* (1953, pp. 145–146, emphasis added)

As this passage makes clear, Easton, like Lasswell, identifies politics as the distribution or allocation of things people want and seek, even as he notes that power/ influence plays a not insignificant role in that process. Dahl's conception of politics in *MPA* leaves him, to some extent, as the odd man out in this trio of renowned political scientists who prominently defined 'politics' in the middle part of the twentieth century.

To recapitulate, unlike other eminent definers of politics (Aristotle, Weber, Lasswell, and Easton), Dahl in *MPA* sees politics as 'the exercise of influence', pure and simple. (Particulars of 'influence', 'power', etc., according to *MPA*, will be addressed below.) This definition of politics unequivocally legitimates political scientists' studying the *politics* of 'private clubs, business firms, labor unions, religious organizations, civic groups, primitive tribes, clans, *perhaps even families*' (1970, p. 6, emphasis added). Indeed, as *MPA* 2nd notes, '[c]ontemporary students of politics do in fact study the political aspects of business firms, labor unions, and other "private" associations' (1970, p. 6). Following *MPA*'s definition of politics, this sort of research is legitimate in its own right and is not to be construed – as Easton would – as useful or legitimate for political scientists only insofar as it sheds light on politics itself. For his part, Easton introduces the term *parapolitics* (or, more precisely, 'parapolitical systems' (1965a, p. 50)) to refer to politics-like activities that do not authoritatively allocate values *for a society*. While Easton concedes that studying the operation of such parapolitical systems can be 'quite helpful' (1965a, p. 51) in understanding politics, he reserves the terms 'politics' and 'political system' for *society-wide* authoritative allocations.

In the first quoted passage in the preceding paragraph, *MPA*'s '*perhaps even* families [emphasis added]' in the list of possible objects for political scientists to study seems a slip. Why 'perhaps'? A prominent, best-selling, and controversial feminist tract by Kate Millett, published in 1969 – after *MPA*'s first edition in 1963 but before *MPA* 2nd appeared in 1970 – explored, among other things, influence or power relationships in heterosexual partnerships. The title, *Sexual Politics* (underscoring added), was fully consistent with *MPA*'s notion of what constituted politics, while *MPA*'s own 'perhaps even families' phrase is not.

Most but not all of Dahl's work addresses *national* political systems. According to *MPA*,

> political scientists and political analysis should – and do – concentrate on what are viewed as *important* instances of politics. That political analysis is more attentive to exercises of influence between the US President and the US Congress than to exercises of influence between Allison and Bill with regard to their Saturday night date is no different from historical analysis being more attentive to, say, Christopher Columbus and Napoleon than to an ordinary sailor on Columbus's ship and ordinary soldier in Napoleon's army. (2003, p. 26)

Dahl's own noteworthy scholarly contributions that do not focus on national political systems include *Who Governs?* (1961), which addresses the politics of one city (New Haven, Connecticut); *Size and Democracy* (coauthored with Edward Tufte) (1973), which analyzes relationships between democratic rule and the population size of subnational (as well as national) units of government; and 'Business and

Politics: A Critical Appraisal of Political Science' (1959), which laments political scientists' paucity of attention to business firms, including their internal 'political order' (1959, p. 5).

Three observations will conclude this section on the influence-centric conception of politics that Dahl embraced over four decades and six editions of *MPA*.

First, discussions of the 'nature of politics' in *MPA* 1st (1963, pp. 7–9) through *MPA* 5th (1991, pp. 5–6) take pains to distinguish politics from economics, and no other social science discipline gets comparable attention. *MPA*'s influence-centric phenomenon of politics is distinguished from the focus of economics on 'scarce resources or the production and distribution of goods and services' (1963, p. 7). In turn, 'democracy' and 'dictatorship' apply to political systems while 'capitalism' and 'socialism' apply to economics. The four possible combinations of these two dichotomous variables are presented in a table (1963, p. 8), accompanied by the observation that whether all four theoretical combinations exist in the real world is an empirical question that bears investigation.

Although *MPA* 6th omits the politics-and-economics treatment appearing in the first five editions, it includes a discussion of how *MPA*'s influence-centric definition of politics easily accommodates the considerable attention that contemporary political scientists pay to big corporations and the enormous influence that they can and do wield. The politics-and-economics material in the first five editions seems an abbreviated and simplified presentation of material presented in Robert Dahl and Charles E. Lindblom, *Politics, Economics, and Welfare* (1953), while *MPA* 6th's treatment of corporations cites and relies on Lindblom's heralded book that appeared a quarter-century later, *Politics and Markets* (1977). The world changes; new understandings of politics and new emphases in political analysis emerge; *MPA* evolves.

Second, despite the prominence of both Easton's delimiting phrase 'the authoritative allocation of values for a society' and of Easton himself (he served as president of the American Political Science Association in 1968–69, two years after Dahl and thirteen years after Lasswell), none of the *MPA* editions mention or cite Easton's formulation, even though it appeared a decade before the publication of the first edition of *MPA*. Several of Easton's other contributions to political analysis, however, are addressed or cited. *MPA* treatments of 'systems' and 'sub-systems' in the second (Dahl, 1970, p. 9n) and all subsequent editions cite Easton's *A Framework for Political Analysis* (1965a) and his *A Systems Analysis of Political Life* (1965b), and the treatments of 'authority' and 'basic and applied research' in *MPA* 6th cite other Easton works (2003, pp. 42n and 148).

Finally, judged by the work of political scientists today, *MPA*'s influence-centric notion of politics has aged well. Consider contemporary political scientists' interest in globalization and non-state actors, not to mention supra-national associations of states such as the European Union. Then consider how tidily or untidily each of these phenomena relates to Easton's 'authoritative allocation of values for a society', Weber's 'territoriality', and Aristotle's 'sovereignty'. With some stretching or tweaking, the Eastonian, Weberian, and Aristotelian notions of politics can probably be made applicable. But Dahl's influence-centric notion of politics easily accommodates these and similar preoccupations of contemporary political scientists, as the discipline continues its decades-long movement away from a singular preoccupation with the politics of states.

ROBERT A. DAHL

Influence and 'influence-terms' such as power, coercion, force, persuasion, and authority

Nowhere in *MPA* is the word *analysis* more literally applicable than in its treatment of what are called 'influence-terms' (1976, p. 25). Through the six *MPA* editions, these core political phenomena are conceptualized, dissected, and assessed to a greater extent than in any of Dahl's other work.

This sustained attention reflects the centrality of 'influence' in Dahl's conception of politics. Unsurprisingly, the treatments of 'influence' and related phenomena evolve – and become more precise – through the six editions, reflecting Dahl's reconceptualization and rethinking in response to relevant scholarly work. By *MPA* 4th (1984), Dahl's initial definition of 'influence' in *MPA* 1st (1963) – 'influence is a *relation among actors* in which one actor induces other actors to act in some way they would not otherwise act' (1963, p. 40, emphasis in original) – gives way to 'influence is a relation among actors such that the wants, desires, preferences, or intentions of one or more actors affect the actions, or predispositions to act, of one or more other actors' (1984, p. 24). In *MPA* 6th, the clarifying words 'human' (actors) and 'in a direction consistent with – and not contrary to – the wants, preferences, or intentions of the influence-wielders' (2003, p. 17) are added. The *MPA* 3rd, 4th, 5th, and 6th definitions of 'influence' (1976, p. 30, 1984, p. 24, 1991, p. 32, 2003, p. 17) are all derived from the work of Jack H. Nagel (1975), a former Yale graduate student who worked with Dahl, and give increasing attention to causation and intentionality in conceptualizing 'influence'.

The evolution and growing precision of *MPA*'s definitions of 'influence' relates to a lament expressed in both the second and third editions. In MPA 2nd, Dahl writes that

> [a]lthough throughout history influence-terms have been central to political analysis, most theorists seem to have assumed, as did Aristotle, that they needed no great elaboration, presumably because their meaning would be clear enough to men of common sense. Even Machiavelli, who was fascinated by the play of power, used a variety of undefined terms to describe and explain political life. In fact, the last several decades have probably witnessed more systematic efforts to tie down these concepts than have the previous millennia of political thought …. As a result there has been a vast improvement in the clarity of the concepts; yet it is still true that different writers do not use influence-terms in the same way: one man's 'influence' is another man's 'power'. (1970, pp. 15–16)

Dahl himself, of course, contributed to the 'vast improvement' in political and other social scientists' understanding of influence-terms. Bibliographic notes ('To Explore Further') appended to the first four editions of *MPA* cite Dahl's fourteen-page *Behavioral Science* article on 'The Concept of Power' (1957) and his elegant and more conceptually sophisticated ten-page entry on 'Power' that appeared eleven years later in the *International Encyclopedia of the Social Sciences* (1968). Along with these two pieces, *MPA*'s treatments of influence and influence-terms, perhaps especially in the 5th and 6th editions, make analytical contributions in their own right as well as synthesizing and, on occasion, critiquing the work of others.

Dahl's varying use of the words 'power' and 'influence' in *MPA*, 'The Concept of Power', and 'Power' may be of particular interest to readers of a journal entitled *The Journal of Political Power*. Perhaps the explanation for the title of Dahl's 'Power' piece (1968) is simply that *Encyclopedia* editor David L. Sills

ROBERT A. DAHL

commissioned Dahl to write a 'power' entry and so that is the term he used. In the piece, Dahl substitutes 'power terms' for *MPA*'s 'influence-terms' and equates 'power' with what he calls 'influence' in *MPA*.

Though less ambitious and perhaps less coherent than his later writings, Dahl's theoretical anchoring in 'The Concept of Power' (1957) mostly parallels that in *MPA* and 'Power' (1968). Consistent with those other writings, 'The Concept' reports 'the long and honorable history attached to such words as power, influence, control, and authority' (1957, p. 202) and notes that

> [s]ome ... readers would doubtless prefer the term 'influence', while others may insist that I am talking about control. I should like to be permitted to use these terms inter-changeably when it is convenient to do so, without denying or seeming to deny that for many other purposes distinctions are necessary and useful. (1957, p. 202)

Then, somewhat at odds with his choice of 'power' to refer to the phenomenon described in his well-known formulation – '*A* has power over *B* to the extent that he can get *B* to do something that *B* would not otherwise do' (1957, pp. 202–203) – Dahl points out that

> in the English language power is an awkward word, for unlike 'influence' and 'con-trol' it has no convenient verb form, nor can the subject and the object of the relation be supplied with noun forms without resort to barbaric neologisms. (1957, p. 202)

Despite the awkwardness and inconvenience of the word 'power' that he notes, Dahl forgoes using 'influence' in its stead.

The bulk of the 'The Concept' proceeds to address how the 'power' of different actors can be compared, starting with formal theorizing and then applying that theorizing to determine the relative power of 34 members of the United States Senate on foreign policy decisions in 1946–54. The empirical application is drawn from a 1956 American Political Science Association conference paper by Dahl and two coauthors (1957, pp. 214–215), which is titled '*Influence* Ranking in the United States Senate' (emphasis added). For reasons unknown and probably unknowable, what was called 'influence' in the 1956 conference paper became 'power' in the 1957 'Concept' article. Perhaps the other coauthors of the paper preferred 'influence'? Perhaps *The Behavioral Scientist* exerted editorial pressure on behalf of 'power'?

As already noted, *MPA* embraces 'influence' as the overarching term to denote human actor(s) intentionally shaping the behavior of other actor(s), and this usage becomes more prominent and clearer as the six editions appear. These things having been said, where does 'power' fit in? Answering this question leads to MPA's treatment of 'forms of influence', which seems to become increasingly systematic, instructive, and penetrating in successive editions of *MPA*.

Not until *MPA* 3rd does the term 'forms of influence' appear, although earlier editions contained seeds of the later and fuller presentations. In *MPA* 3rd, 4th, and 5th, 'forms of influence' are said to highlight differences in the means by which influence is exercised (1976, p. 44, 1984, p. 38, 1991, p. 39). In *MPA* 6th, 'forms of influence distinguish among various *hows* and *whys* of influence' (2003, p. 38, emphases in the original). All the 'forms' of influence have equal ontological standing as instances of influence, but variation in the form of influence has 'important practical and moral consequences' (2003, p. 38).

39

MPA 6th identifies seven forms of influence: *inducement, power, force, coercion, persuasion, manipulation,* and *authority* (2003, pp. 38–43). More important than the labels for these various 'forms of influence' are *MPA*'s instructive distinctions in the ways influence can be exerted. Influence-wielders can employ rewards ('inducement') or sanctions or deprivations ('power'); use physical means such as lifting, pushing, or even shooting ('force') or the threat of force ('coercion', which is 'an extreme variant of power' (2003, p. 40)); or rely exclusively on rational and truthful communication ('persuasion' or, in some *MPA* editions, 'rational persuasion') or on intentionally false and misleading communication ('manipulation'). Finally, influence can be wielded via 'authority', which in *MPA* consists of automatic, habitual, almost unthinking responsiveness to the influence-wielder's preferences. As *MPA* 6th notes, one basis for authority is the perception by the actor over whom influence is wielded 'that it would be proper, right, or morally good ... to obey' (2003, p. 60). Such authority, said to stem from 'legitimacy', is 'especially efficient and attractive to' influence-wielders (2003, p. 60), and perhaps to those who are influenced as well.

The *MPA* 5th preface states that the treatment of influence (Dahl writes 'power and influence', but may well mean 'influence' or at least mostly 'influence') 'has been a pivotal feature of the book from the first edition onward' (1991, p. xi). This claim is undeniable. As noted earlier, *MPA*'s identification of influence as the essence of politics distinguishes Dahl from the likes of Aristotle, Weber, Easton, and even Lasswell. *MPA*'s greatest analytical contributions probably lie, however, in its conceptual and systematic treatment of 'influence-terms' and how influence is exercised at both micro- and macro-levels.

MPA emphasizes that how and why influence is wielded matters greatly, both empirically (e.g. the likelihood that a political regime or a particular leader will survive and continue to be a major wielder of influence) and normatively (e.g. the morality of the use of different forms of influence in particular circumstances – to use a prominent contemporary example, the application of physical force or coercion to suspected terrorists). *MPA* argues that a preference for rational persuasion above all other forms of influence (what *MPA* calls 'the *absolute principle* of rational persuasion' (1991, 47, emphasis in the original)) is not always compelling and that would-be adherents of this principle need to rethink the matter:

> a notion of mutual influence based on rational persuasion lies often half-hidden in the heart of many conceptions of an ideal society .... Yet no large number of persons has ever interacted over an extended period of time in and outside their group without developing [and using?] means [i.e. forms] of influence other than persuasion .... the absolute principle of rational persuasion never can be upheld until it is always adhered to by everyone .... Agreement by rational persuasion for some persons can mean coercion for others .... (1991, pp. 46–47).

In the later editions of *MPA*, the special standing of authority as a form of influence is emphasized. *MPA* 6th declares that 'authority is arguably the most desirable and most important form of influence' and notes Dahl's long-time colleague (and sometimes coauthor) Charles E. Lindblom's contention that 'politics itself boils down to a struggle for authority among competing political actors' (2003, p. 41).

Probably more than other forms of influence, 'authority is often connected to other forms of influence' (2003, p. 43). Past use of force can make coercion or power more likely to be successful, past use of persuasion may make manipulation

ROBERT A. DAHL

more likely to succeed, and past use of most or even all the other forms of influence can pave the way for authority (in the *MPA* sense of automatic or habitual obedience).

Influence and interests; 'levels of influence'

Two analytical angles on influence that receive greater attention in later *MPA* editions are the relationship between 'influence' and 'interests' and the different 'levels' at which influence can be exercised or exerted. To a considerable extent, these treatments seem to be responses to prominent critiques by Peter Bachrach and Morton S. Baratz (1962) and Steven Lukes (1974) of Dahl's celebrated study of 'democracy and power' in New Haven, Connecticut (1961).

MPA's stance on 'influence' and 'interests' can be summarized thus: The concept of influence is best defined without resort to the concept of interests. The 'wants, desires, preferences, or intentions' (2003, p. 17) of the actors involved – the influence-wielder(s) and person(s) being influenced – are *the* key factors in determining whether influence has occurred, *not* these individuals' 'interests'. Moreover, a satisfactory definition of influence 'without resort to interest … does not prevent us from analyzing potentially important connections between influence and interests' (2003, pp. 16–17). In an uncharacteristic passage, *MPA* explicitly critiques and rejects Lukes's reliance on 'interests' in his definition of 'power' (for *MPA*, 'influence'): 'Lukes's proposed definition runs into several serious difficulties … [and] seems rather arbitrary as well' (2003, p. 15).[3]

An analytical highlight of *MPA* 5th and 6th is the treatment of 'spheres of decision-making or levels of influence' (2003, pp. 45–48). Earlier editions do not address this topic to any significant extent, but *MPA* 5th and 6th distinguish four 'levels' of decision-making at which influence can be wielded: that is, influencing another actor or actors in the context of (1) options from an already formed agenda of choices, (2) the 'composition of the agenda [of options] itself' (2003, p. 45), (3) change or preservation of the very 'structures' that construct agendas of options (a diverse set of examples of such 'structures' is offered, including 'family arrangements, tribes, … kinship systems, … political parties, universities, legislatures, corporations, and … much broader systems such as democratic or authoritarian regimes, market and nonmarket economies' (2003, p. 46), and (4) the way others think about the world around them, i.e. 'their awareness or "consciousness"' (2003, p. 47).[4]

The four-level framework in *MPA* 6th can be seen as Dahl's last word in response to the many searching critiques of his *Who Governs? Democracy and Power in an American City* (1961), which first appeared 42 years before *MPA* 6th was published.[5] Politics – that is, influence – and associated decision-making can be understood to operate on four different levels, with the reach of influence likely to be broader and more consequential as one progresses from levels 1 through 4. All this is presented in *MPA* 6th in less than four pages and introduced by the cautionary words that

> [t]he distinctions we are about to explore can be challenging to those who do not ordinarily think in such terms, but contemporary political scientists generally agree that such distinctions can be vitally important in political analysis. (2003, p. 45)

ROBERT A. DAHL

While *MPA*'s concise treatment cannot completely flesh out each level or explore every serious objection, it nevertheless seems characteristic of Dahl at his best: integrating the contributions of others with his own core insights about a topic and presenting them in straightforward, commonsensical language, together with examples that usefully illustrate conceptual and theoretical points.

Government and the state; corporations

Government and the state, staples of traditional political analysis, are not overlooked in *MPA*, despite its influence-centric conception of politics. Nor are corporations.

In discussing his 'authoritative allocation of values for a society' conception of politics, Easton writes that 'neither the concept of the state nor that of power is satisfactory even as a rough approximation' (Easton 1953, p. 126). I earlier directed attention to the 'nor that of power' part of the quotation; now I want to focus on Easton's characterization of 'the state' as an unsatisfactory focus for political analysis and an unsatisfactory element in defining politics. I am not the first to suggest that Easton's formulation may have pushed 'the state' out the front door, so to speak, only to let it return through the back door. To the extent that most, perhaps nearly all, society-wide 'authoritative allocations' come from governments, government and the state seem to remain central to Easton's notion of politics.

MPA's influence-centric definition of politics seems to have no such front door/back door problems. According to all six editions of *MPA*, the 'government' of a state '*successfully upholds a claim to the exclusive regulation of the legitimate use of physical force in enforcing its rules within a given territorial area*' (1963, p. 12, emphasis in the original).[6] Armed with an influence-centric definition of politics and a Weberian notion of government, political scientists can and should pay considerable attention to governments because, as *MPA* notes, governments exercise considerable influence. But *MPA*'s conception of politics also allows for political analysis of entities other than governments on account of the influence that they wield: churches, labor unions, secret societies, families, and, perhaps especially, modern corporations. According to Charles E. Lindblom, governments and big corporations share a 'duality of leadership' in modern industrial societies such as the United States because they 'each exercise preponderant amounts of influence' (Lindblom 1977 cited Dahl 2003, p. 33). In turn, both governments *and* big corporations are appropriate and important subjects for political analysis because of the amounts of influence they exercise.

MPA, Journal of Political Power, *and words about words*[7]

MPA's definition and treatment of 'influence-terms', 'forms of influence', and 'politics' relate to both the very subject of this journal – 'political power' – as well as its 'Aims and Scope' (2013). *MPA* 2nd notes that 'one man's "influence" is another man's "power"' (1970, p. 16) and, as already noted, in writings other than *MPA* Dahl himself has used the two terms interchangeably. If politics is 'the exercise of influence' and 'influence' is *MPA*'s term for what others and Dahl himself in other places call 'power', then the term 'political power' seems problematic in the context of *MPA*'s conceptual and terminological framework.

ROBERT A. DAHL

For one thing, 'political power' can be seen to constitute a redundancy parallel to *MPA*'s occasional – and, given its own terminological framework, regrettable – use of the term 'political influence'. *MPA* 3rd and 4th each contain chapters entitled 'Political Influence', and *MPA* 1st and *MPA* 5th identify two 'similarities' among political systems thus: '*Some members of the political system seek to gain influence over the policies, rules, and decisions enforced by the government—i.e., political influence*' and '*Political influence is distributed unevenly among adult members of a political system*' (1963, p. 16; 1991, p. 53. *MPA* 5th (1991) substitutes 'the' for 'adult'. Emphasis in the original).

If politics is '*the exercise of influence*' (2003, p. 24, emphasis in the original), then what can '*political* influence' be, other than an inadvertent redundancy?

Is the term 'political power' in the title of this journal also a redundancy? Is there such a phenomenon as *non*-political power? Yes, 'electrical power', according to the *Journal of Political Power* 2011 editorial explaining the addition of 'political' to the journal's previous name, *Journal of Power* (Haugaard 2010, p. 1).

The term 'political power' can raise another concern, the occurrence of power (or influence) relations involving non-human actors, a complication that *MPA* addresses:

> There is general agreement that influence-terms refer to relationships among human beings. In ordinary language, I may speak of man's power over nature or my power over my dog; a theologian may speak of God's power, or divine influence on events. But in political analysis, influence-terms are usually restricted to relationships among human actors. (1970, p. 16, 1976, p. 29, 1984, p. 23. The 1976 and 1984 editions omit 'In ordinary language'.)

MPA 3rd, 4th, and *5th* all suggest use of the word 'social' to limit 'influence' to human-to-human relationships, which, to be sure, hardly seems an ideal terminological solution (1976, p. 30n, 1984, p. 24n, 1991, p. 28). But this *Journal*'s resort to '*political* power' seems no better, especially if the rationale is that 'in post-structuralist theory the realm of the political has become extended to encompass *social* life in general' (2011, p. 2, emphasis added). If so, why not follow *MPA*'s suggestion and use the term '*social* power'?

Does the term 'political power' convey that the phenomenon of interest is limited to instances of *human* or *human-related* power? Perhaps, indeed probably so. Then again, with tongue firmly in cheek, perhaps 'non-electrical power' is the preferable terminological option. But even such wording runs afoul of the phrase 'power of a [non-electrical] storm'.

All this having been said, Dahl would doubtless agree with Mark Haugaard's point that 'it is important not to make a fetish out of specific words: they are simply conceptual tools which enable us to order [and understand] the wor[l]d' (2011, p. 1). Even so, words, precisely and consistently used, are critically important elements in political analysis. *MPA*'s careful exposition of the various 'forms of influence' is commendable; *MPA*'s use of 'political influence' is not.

This discussion of the redundancy or possible redundancy embodied in 'political influence' and 'political power' calls to mind a related terminological miscue sometimes appearing in political analysis: The use of 'political' when 'governmental' would be more precise and is probably intended. Consider the following institutions that exercise influence in modern societies: families, churches, legislatures, social or fraternal organizations, courts, and corporations. MPA's influence-centric notion

43

of politics justifies all these properly being called 'political institutions', but only 'legislatures' and 'courts' can rightly be labelled 'governmental institutions'. In the first *MPA* 'similarity' among political systems quoted above – 'Some members of the political system seek to gain influence over the policies, rules, and decisions enforced by the government – i.e. political influence' (1991, p. 53) – '*governmental* influence' would be preferable because it both avoids the redundancy of '*political* influence' and provides greater analytical precision. Distinguishing non-governmental influence-wielding institutions from governmental ones is hardly trivial in the context of 'ordering [and understanding] the world' around us.

The *Journal of Political Power*'s statement of 'Aims and Scope' (2013) notes the 'the fundamental contrast between those who view power negatively, as domination, and those who think of it positively, as an essential ingredient of autonomy and empowerment'. With respect to this duality, *MPA* repeatedly asserts (in all six editions, with only slight variation in wording) that its 'definition says nothing at all about human *motives*' (1963, p. 7, emphasis in original). Individuals may or may not seek influence 'driven by deep inner needs to rule others' or by other particular motives (2003, p. 25), and *MPA* professes to take no stand on whether the phenomenon of 'influence' is to be viewed positively or negatively, even while making clear that different *forms* of influence have different moral standing.[8]

Differences and similarities among political systems

Each edition of *MPA* has two chapters on 'Similarities' and 'Differences' in political systems. While *MPA*'s approach to the nature of politics and 'influence terms' is mostly conceptual and theoretical, it treats similarities and differences among political systems more empirically. The Similarities and Differences chapters serve as the preludes to *MPA*'s overview of Dahl's well-known work on democracy and polyarchy.

The close similarity of all six *MPA* editions' Similarities and Differences chapters, especially the nearly identical versions in *MPA* 3rd through *MPA* 6th, seems a departure from usual *MPA* edition-to-edition revising norms. In all but *MPA* 1st, the Similarities chapters begin with the 'ruling class' views of Mosca, Pareto, and Michels. The Differences chapters all observe that there are many ways to distinguish political systems from one another and present Aristotle's well-known 2×3 classification scheme as well as Max Weber's identification of three kinds of legitimacy that can be claimed by leaders of a political system. To reinforce the point that 'thousands of criteria' (1976, p. 71, 1984, p. 66) can be used to construct 'typologies', *MPA* 3rd and 4th both report that 'at the Seventh World Congress of the International Political Association in 1967, entire sessions were devoted to the topic "Typologies of Political Systems"' (1976, pp. 69–70, 1984, p. 64) and cite a number of relevant data sources and classification schemes. But every edition of *MPA* makes clear that, while 'whole new collections of data … on national political systems' (1984, p. 63) became available beginning in the 1960s, 'schemes for classifying political systems are … as old as the study of politics itself' (1984, p. 64).

Unsurprisingly, all six *MPA* editions' presentation of insights and observations about political systems centers on the politics of states. This focus reflects the history of political science, of course, although in the half-century since the appearance of *MPA* 1st the discipline's concentration on national political systems has somewhat lessened. As already noted, *MPA*'s influence-centric conception of

ROBERT A. DAHL

politics and political systems legitimates the study of politics (i.e. 'the exercise of influence') in entities as diverse as national and subnational governments, business firms, labor unions, families, and romantic liaisons.

How does *MPA* handle this disparity between the breadth of its influence-centric conception of politics in earlier chapters and its later concentration on the political systems of states? Somewhat briefly in earlier editions and with somewhat greater length and explicitness in later editions.

At the outset of its Similarities chapter, *MPA* 1st notes that the 'empirical regularities' in political systems to be addressed 'occur not only in states and governments but also in trade unions, business firms, clubs, cities, and other political systems' (1963, p. 14). Anthropological research finding that 'the Zuni Indians of the Southwest lacked virtually any striving for power' (1963, p. 16) is presented as an exception to the 'regularity' that some members of a political system inevitably seek to gain control over the government. Moreover, commentary on the 'regularity' that a political system is affected by the existence of other political systems (that is, 'every political system engages in *foreign relations*') notes that '[e]ven a club or a religious congregation cannot act with complete autonomy; and the leaders of a trade union must take into account the past or probable actions of business firms, other unions, and the government' (1963, p. 22, 1970, p. 44, 1976, p. 64, 1984, p. 58, 1991, p. 57, 2003, p. 63. Emphasis in the original in 1963 and 1970; 'even' is omitted in 2003). But these examples are exceptions: *MPA* examples of empirical regularities among political systems come mostly from national political systems.

MPA 2nd, 3rd, and 4th all note the 'the broad definition of "political system"' that they have adopted (1970, p. 36, 1976, p. 55, 1984, p. 49) and continue thus:

> Our systematic knowledge extends to only a small portion of a tiny number of these systems. Political science advances, by and large, through the specialized study of particular types of political systems (1970, p. 36, 1976, p. 56, 1984, p. 50), such as the political institutions of a particular country, as in the study of American government; or of several countries, as in the study of comparative politics; or in the relationships between countries, as in the study of international relations .... (1970, p. 36)

MPA 5th takes the matter further:

> Strange as it may seem, some highly important political systems have not usually been studied by political scientists (or for the most part other social scientists) *as political systems* with relations of power and institutions for governing. Notable among these are the organizations within which people spend most of their daily lives: workplaces, business firms, economic enterprises. Nor have political scientists paid much attention to the diminutive political system within which people spend most of the rest of their daily lives – the family. What political scientists (and political philosophers) have focused on over many centuries is a small subset of political systems of truly extraordinary importance: those involved, more or less directly, in governing the state. (1991, p. 50, emphasis in original)

MPA 6th essentially repeats the foregoing quote from MPA 5th and adds that political scientists have mostly concentrated on '**national political systems**' (2003, p. 56, bold print in the original).

ROBERT A. DAHL

This observation that political analysis has mostly focused on national political systems is certainly warranted. Yet *MPA* does not pursue to any extent how to compare or approach the relative importance of national political systems and the 'diminutive' political systems amidst which most people spend most of their lives – workplaces, families, romantic relationships. The *MPA* 5th quotation presented above simply asserts the 'truly extraordinary importance' of national political systems.

The early chapters of every edition of *MPA* present a useful way to think about comparing the relative influence of different actors. *MPA*'s notions of 'scope' – 'the matter over which an actor has influence' (2003, p. 19) – and 'domain' – 'the persons over whom an actor has influence' – (2003, p. 19) would likely be good starting points for considering which of the 'millions' of existing political systems (1970, p. 36) are indeed most influential in people's lives. One can both commend *MPA* for explicitly recognizing the long-time preoccupation of political analysis with national political systems and regret that it does not undertake to compare and contrast, at least in a preliminary way, the relative impact of the *millions* of different political systems that envelop human beings.

Democracy and polyarchy

On which of Dahl's lifetime of insights and perspectives about democracy and polyarchy does *MPA* focus in treating these two central concerns of political science? To what extent do the emphases change in the six editions of *MPA*?

Chapters on democracy and polyarchy in all six *MPA*'s editions single out two forms of influence, coercion and persuasion, both addressed earlier in the books, and make a number of different yet related points about them. After noting a 'profound though not uncommon misunderstanding about popular governments – about "democracies" – to assume that they do not employ coercion. They do'. (1963, p. 76), *MPA* 1st explains how popular government institutions are associated with lessening 'the need for coercion and increase the prospects for peaceful adjustment' (1963, p. 77). *MPA* 2nd observes that some types of coercion 'are excluded or minimized in polyarchies *by definition*. A regime that imprisons the leaders of all opposition parties or suppresses critical newspapers, for example, is by definition not a polyarchy' (1970, p. 62, emphasis in original). Yet *MPA* 2nd also makes the case that the lower incidence of coercion in polyarchies is not simply a matter of definition. (Perhaps the 'profound though not uncommon misunderstanding' about coercion and democracies reported in *MPA* 1st is a consequence of the exclusion, by definition, of 'some types of coercion' in democratic political systems?) *MPA* 3rd through *MPA* 6th assert that 'in polyarchies, as opposed to hegemonies, political [from the context, *government* is probably intended] leaders rely more on persuasion and less on coercion' (1976, p. 83, 1984, p. 79, 1991, p. 78, 2003, p. 85). In *MPA* 5th and 6th, wherein the fullest accounts of Dahl's thinking on democracy and polyarchy appear, the priority afforded persuasion over coercion is identified as a 'further difference between polyarchies and nonpolyarchies' (1991, pp. 75, 78–79, 2003, pp. 81, 85–86), even while not being part of the definitional essence of polyarchies.

What about the incidence of governments' use of other forms of influence in polyarchies and non-polyarchies? Are persuasion and manipulation more prevalent in democratic or non-democratic regimes? What about inducement? Do political actors in polyarchies – government leaders, candidates for government office, voters and would-be campaign contributors – engage more or less frequently than political actors in non-polyarchies in offering rewards to shape other political actors' behavior? And, perhaps most importantly, does the incidence of authority as a form of influence, especially by government leaders, vary systematically across polyarchies and non-polyarchies? *MPA* does not address these empirical questions. Nor does it enter into related or parallel normative inquiries: Is widespread and effective authority in a political system – in which actors 'automatically' obey government leaders – good or bad? Perhaps the answer depends on what generates the automatic acquiescence that characterizes *MPA*'s notion of authority – legitimacy based on the perceived 'moral rightness' of the regime, *or* fear of adverse consequences such as the application of physical force for failure to fall into line. Of course, the authority of governments in most or even all national political systems stems from a mix of such factors. These and related questions are not addressed to any extent in *MPA*.

MPA 1st and *MPA* 2nd each devote one chapter to democracy and polyarchy, and *MPA* 1st presents two questions to frame the analysis:

(1) What kinds of conditions tend to reduce the use of coercion in a political system?
(2) What conditions favor the peaceful adjustment of conflicts in a polyarchal system? (1963, p. 73).

While these two questions do not appear in *MPA* 2nd, the outline of the analysis remains mostly similar. *MPA* 1st notes 'a strong relationship between popular government and abundance' (1963, p. 81) and presents figures showing 'telephones per 1000 persons', 'per-capita income', and 'percentage literate' drawn from Seymour M. Lipset's well-known *Political Man*, which was published in 1960 (1963, pp. 82–83). Considerable discussion of 'psychological dispositions' (1963, p. 87ff), which draws on work by Harold Lasswell and Richard Hofstadter, among others, also appears. *MPA* 2nd introduces cross-national data and analyses on incidence of conflict, with the 1969 *Report to the* [US] *National Commission on the Causes and Prevention of Violence* serving as a key source (1970, pp. 63–66). The 'abundance' analysis appears again, but the treatment of 'psychological dispositions' does not.

'Political Regimes: Popular and Hegemonic' is the title of the chapter on democracy and polyarchy in *MPA* 3rd and 4th and seems to be a transition to the fuller and different treatments of polyarchies and non-polyarchies that appear in *MPA* 5th and 6th. In his preface to *MPA* 5th, Dahl heralds 'the most comprehensive revision I have undertaken' (1991, p. xi). One result is a doubling of the number of *MPA* chapters on popular government, and chapters titled 'Differences: Polyarchies and Nonpolyarchies' and 'Polyarchies and Nonpolyarchies: An Explanation' appear in both *MPA* 5th and *MPA* 6th. The two chapters in *MPA* 6th update the *MPA* 5th data and analysis but follow the same general approach.

The first of the two chapters on polyarchy in *MPA* 5th and 6th summarize the history of democracy and polyarchy. Polyarchy – popular government as practiced in such contemporary democratic political systems as the United States, Britain, Norway, India, and Japan – emerged when the notion of 'representation' reshaped the theory and practice of popular government, which had previously been conditioned – and confined – by the ancient Greek and Roman experiences with direct democracy. Graphs present data on the growth of polyarchy from 1850 to the time of publication, showing both absolute numbers and percentages of countries practicing polyarchy (*MPA* 5th, pp. 76–77, *MPA* 6th, pp. 82–83). The percentages have tended to remain relatively stable in contrast to the absolute numbers of polyarchies and of sovereign nations, both of which have grown rapidly since about 1960.

MPA 5th and 6th next identify seven institutions that characterize contemporary popular government or 'polyarchy'. Similar lists appear in earlier as well as later work by Dahl (1982, pp. 10–11, 1998, pp. 85–86), although with slightly different emphases and numbering. (In Dahl (1998), two of the seven elements appearing in *MPA* 5th and 6th are combined into one, making for a total of six.) The seven polyarchal institutions include control of government policy by officials chosen in frequent, fair, and non-coercive elections and related phenomena such as freedom of expression, the press, and association as well as citizens' access to diverse sources of information. Besides the seven institutions, *MPA* 5th and 6th identify what are labelled 'further differences between polyarchies and nonpolyarchies' (1991, pp. 75ff, 2003, pp. 81ff). Polyarchies are said to be likely to protect civil rights and liberties above and beyond those that are necessary or definitional characteristics, enjoy a 'pluralist' sphere of relatively autonomous groups and organizations, and, as addressed above, have government leaders relying more on persuasion than coercion (1991, 78–80, 2003, pp. 84–86).

The *MPA* 5th and 6th chapters entitled 'Polyarchies and Nonpolyarchies: An Explanation' address why 'some countries have developed and sustained the institutions of polyarchy while others have not' (1991, p. 81). *MPA* 6th's answer comes in five parts that are adapted from Dahl's *Democracy and Its Critics* (1989): (1) 'Subordination of the Military', (2) 'A Supportive Political Culture', (3) 'A Modern, Dynamic, Pluralist Society', (4) the extent of subcultural diversity and how subcultural differences have been handled, and (5) the presence or absence of external interference (2003, Chapter 9, pp. 88–100).

MPA's coverage of polyarchy and related matters is noticeably more structured and more comprehensive in the 5th and 6th editions, although, of course, even two chapters are hardly sufficient to explore every analytical and empirical nook and cranny. Emphases include both how contemporary popular governments, i.e. polyarchies, differ and indeed must differ from the early Greek and Roman models, and how and when the notion of 'representation' aided the reemergence of popular government in its contemporary form, 'polyarchy'. Also presented are the seven 'institutions' that constitute the essential attributes of contemporary popular government, as well as a few other characteristics typically appearing in polyarchies today. Finally, five factors explaining why some countries have polyarchies and others do not summarize Dahl's thinking on a central concern of modern political analysis. Presumably, *MPA* 5th and 6th present what Dahl saw as most significant for understanding popular government, the subject on which he focused during his long and extraordinarily distinguished career.

A primer for modern political analysis

MPA presents Dahl's views on how contemporary political analysis proceeds and ought to proceed, identifying what to study – politics, the exercise of influence – and how to conceptualize and analyze that which is studied. Delving into

ROBERT A. DAHL

similarities and differences among political systems, *MPA* addresses democracy and polyarchy, Dahl's primary preoccupation during his scholarly career.

For Dahl, 'basic concepts, ideas, and analytical tools' are essential for good political analysis (*MPA* 1963, p. viii). A sizable part of an *MPA* 3rd chapter entitled 'What Is Political Analysis?' is devoted to distinguishing and addressing empirical, normative, policy, and semantic (or conceptual) 'orientations' (1976, Chapter 3, pp. 12–20). While that somewhat unwieldy quartet appearing in the third edition is mentioned only in passing in *MPA* 4th (1984, pp. 4–5) and essentially disappears in the two last editions, *MPA* very much reflects the instructive blend of conceptual, empirical, and normative analyses that characterizes and enriches Dahl's corpus of scholarly work.

These are the essentials of *MPA and* of modern political analysis according to Robert A. Dahl: Politics is the exercise of influence, an umbrella term for key phenomena such as power, persuasion, inducement, force, coercion, manipulation, and authority. Political systems exhibit important similarities and differences, including, most significantly, whether they are polyarchies or non-polyarchies. These foci should and do anchor modern political analysis. Whatever happens, 'the concepts … set out here will remain helpful, perhaps indispensable, for understanding the world in which we live' (2003, p. 32).

Disclosure statement

Bruce Stinebrickner is the co-author (with Robert A. Dahl) of *MPA* 6th (2003).

Notes

1. When an identical or almost identical point or passage appears in more than one edition of MPA, to reduce the repeated distraction of multiple citations I shall generally cite only one edition. When the context seems to make it useful or even necessary, citations of more than one *MPA* edition will appear.
2. As coauthor of the sixth edition of *MPA*, I was responsible for initial drafting of the revised manuscript, but Dahl and I discussed all significant changes in advance of my drafting. He carefully and promptly read every chapter I drafted and suggested changes that he thought were warranted. This article will treat *MPA* 6th as Dahl's work and essentially ignore the existence of a coauthor for that edition. In turn, I shall in places be offering criticisms of my own work in *MPA* 6th, which, of course, is consistent with the approach that Dahl took to *his* own work over his entire career. I am also pleased to report that Bob Dahl was a wonderful coauthor – as conscientious, accommodating, and gracious as anyone could wish for.
3. This criticism of Lukes's approach is one of *MPA*'s infrequent explicit and direct critiques of other scholars' work. In this context, Dahl's comments about responding to criticisms of his work that were recorded in interviews conducted in 1980 and 1981 seem worth noting: 'I decided early on that I didn't want to spend my time dealing with all the criticisms of any work [of mine]. One view is that you have a scholarly obligation to continue the discussion because that's a part of progress in the field. I, for a whole variety of reasons, have not wanted to do that…. It may be that I've done less of that than I'm properly obliged to do' ('Robert A. Dahl', 1991, p. 176).
4. Mapping or trying to map *MPA*'s four 'levels of influence' onto Clegg's distinctions among episodic, dispositional, and systemic power (1989 cited Haugaard 2010), or vice versa, might well be an interesting and productive exercise, but it is beyond the scope of this article.

ROBERT A. DAHL

5. Characterizing the 'spheres of decision-making or levels of influence' discussion in *MPA* 6th as Dahl's 'last word in response in to … critiques' should be read in the context of Dahl's professed disinclination to engage in that sort of enterprise. See Note 3.
6. In *MPA*, a 'state' consists of a 'government' and the residents of the territory ruled by that government (*MPA* 6th, p. 31). Stephanie Lawson's article (1993) conceptualizing *state*, *regime*, and *government* suggests that political scientists studying comparative and international politics typically have understandings that diverge somewhat from *MPA* s use of these terms. But these terminological differences do not undermine *MPA* s attributing central importance to government and the state in politics. I am grateful to my departmental colleague Brett O'Bannon for calling this matter to my attention and for directing me to Lawson's article.
7. Dahl uses the phrase 'Words About Words' as his heading for short explanations about the use and meaning of particular words that appear, set off from the main text, throughout his On Democracy (1998). For that reason, its use in a subheading in th s article seems particularly apt.
8. According to Haugaard (p. 432, 2010), *MPA*'s neutral stance is consistent with the 'sociological analytic political science' approach to influence/power and is by no means idiosyncratic.

References

Aims and scope, 2013. *Journal of Political Power*, 6 (3), inside back cover.

Bachrach, P. and Baratz, M.S., 1962. Two faces of power. *American Political Science Review*, 56, 947–952.

Dahl, R.A., 1957. The concept of power. *Behavioral Science*, 2 (3), 201–215.

Dahl, R.A., 1959. Business and politics: a critical appraisal of political science. *In*: R.A. Dahl, M. Haire, and P.F. Lazarsfeld, eds. *Social science research on business: product and potential*. New York: Columbia University Press, 1–44.

Dahl, R.A., 1961. *Who governs? Democracy and power in an American city*. New Haven, CT: Yale University Press.

Dahl, R.A., 1963. *Modern political analysis*. Englewood Cliffs, NJ: Prentice-Hall.

Dahl, R.A., 1968. Power. *In*: D.L. Sills, ed. *International encyclopedia of the social sciences*. Vol. 12. New York, NY: Macmillan and Free Press, 405–415.

Dahl, R.A., 1970. *Modern political analysis*. 2nd ed. Englewood Cliffs, NJ: Prentice-Hall.

Dahl, R.A., 1976. *Modern political analysis*. 3rd ed. Englewood Cliffs, NJ: Prentice-Hall.

Dahl, R.A., 1982. *Dilemmas of pluralist democracy: autonomy vs. control*. New Haven, CT: Yale University Press.

Dahl, R.A., 1984. *Modern political analysis*. 4th ed. Englewood Cliffs, NJ: Prentice-Hall.

Dahl, R.A., 1989. *Democracy and its critics*. New Haven, CT: Yale University Press.

Dahl, R.A., 1991. *Modern Political Analysis*. 5th ed. Englewood Cliffs, NJ: Prentice-Hall.

Dahl, R.A., 1998. *On democracy*. New Haven, CT: Yale University Press.

Dahl, R.A. and Stinebrickner, B., 2003. *Modern political analysis*. 6th ed. Upper Saddle River, NJ: Prentice Hall.

Dahl, R.A. and Tufte, E.R., 1973. *Size and democracy*. Stanford, CA: Stanford University Press.

Easton, D., 1953. *The political system: an inquiry into the state of political science*. New York: Alfred A. Knopf.

Easton, D., 1965a. *A framework for political analysis*. Englewood Cliffs, NJ: Prentice-Hall.

ROBERT A. DAHL

Easton, D., 1965b. *A systems analysis of political life*. New York: Wiley.

Haugaard, Mark, 2010. Power: a 'family resemblance' concept. *European Journal of Cultural Studies*, 13 (4), 419–438.

Haugaard, M., 2011. Editorial. *Journal of Political Power*, 4 (1), 1–8.

Lasswell, H.D., 1936. *Politics: who gets what, when, how*. New York: The World.

Lasswell, H.D. and Kaplan, A., 1950. *Power and society: a framework for political inquiry*. New Haven, CT: Yale University Press.

Lawson, S., 1993. Conceptual issues in the comparative study of regime change and democratization. *Comparative Politics*, 25 (2), 183–205.

Lindblom, C.E., 1977. *Politics and markets: the world's political-economic systems*. New York, NY: Basic Books.

Lukes, S., 1974. *Power, a radical view*. London: Macmillan.

Martin, D., 2014. Robert A. Dahl dies at 98; defined politics and power. *The New York Times*, 8 Feb, p. A16, 5.

Nagel, J.H., 1975. *The descriptive analysis of power*. New Haven, CT: Yale University Press.

'Robert A. Dahl', 1991. (Edited transcript of an interview between Robert A. Dahl and Nelson Polsby) *In*: M.A. Baer, M.E. Jewell, and L. Sigelman, 1991, eds. *Political Science in America: Oral Histories of a Discipline*. Lexington, KY: University Press of Kentucky, pp. 166–178.

Misinterpreting Dahl on power

David A. Baldwin

Columbia University, New York and Department of Political Science Woodrow Wilson School, Princeton University, Princeton, USA

Dahl's critics have often called attention to important aspects of power relations – e.g. the suppression of issues and consciousness control. The critics, however, have not always portrayed Dahl's views as accurately as one might wish. Distinguishing between an abstract concept of power and operational definitions adopted for purposes of specific research projects is fundamental for Dahl. Furthermore, Dahl's concept of power implies nothing about the preferences of B, is not zero-sum, does not necessitate compulsion, may or may not be subtle or visible, is not confined to material resources, and may be either direct and immediate or indirect and long term.

Robert Dahl's writings on power have been both very influential and repeatedly criticized. The critics, however, have not always portrayed Dahl's views as accurately as one might wish. This essay will review the roots of this criticism and examine some examples of misinterpretations of Dahl's concept of power. It has become commonplace to begin a study of power with references to Dahl's 'The Concept of Power' (1957), his *Who Governs?* (1961), and/or the controversy that followed – usually dubbed 'the community power debate'.[1] This essay will therefore begin with an overview of these works and the ensuing 'debate', which continued into the 1970s. The essay will conclude with an examination of a number of misinterpretations of Dahl's concept of power.

Dahl and his critics

Dahl's (1957) definition of power in terms of A's ability to get B to do something that B would not otherwise do has been both widely accepted and widely criticized.[2] Although alternative definitions abound, none has been so widely accepted as this one; and none has attracted so many critics. Familiarity with the principal foci of the debate between Dahl and his critics provides necessary background for understanding modern power analysis.[3] The most important source of criticism of Dahl's work on power was labeled 'the community power debate'. The discussion below will focus on the two most influential sources of criticism – an article by (Bachrach and Baratz 1962) and a pamphlet by Lukes (1974). Following that, some misinterpretations of Dahl's approach to the study of power will be examined.

ROBERT A. DAHL

'The Concept of Power'

Dahl's 1957 article, 'The Concept of Power', is the most influential article ever written on the subject. Pettit (2008) views it as a 'classic paper on power [that] remains relevant and useful ... in contemporary discussion'. The call for papers for the 2006 Annual Meeting of the American Political Science Association recognized the importance of the article by citing the approaching 50-year anniversary of its publication and announcing that the theme of the meeting would be power. Rae (1988, p. 24) observes that 'the modern history of "power" in US political science begins with the elegant construction in Dahl's 1957 paper'. The latter statement, however, may go too far inasmuch as it fails to acknowledge the seminal contributions by Lasswell and Kaplan (1950), Simon (1953), and March (1955, 1955) before 1957–not to mention the contribution by Dahl and Lindblom in their magisterial *Politics, Economics, and Welfare* (1953).

The paper has only ten published references, four of which acknowledge social psychology and game theory as alternative approaches to the study of power and one referring to Weber's distinction between power and authority. The remaining five references are to works by Lasswell and Kaplan, March, and Simon. The sole footnote refers to the 'seminal influence' of Lasswell on the study of power 'by demonstrating the importance of concepts such as power and influence, particularly in political analysis, and by insisting upon rigorous conceptual clarity'. He notes that March and Simon use an approach similar to that of Lasswell and Kaplan. It is worth noting these references, since they seem to have escaped the attention of many of Dahl's subsequent critics.

In addition to offering a definition of power, the paper discusses the properties of power relations, the difficulty of power comparisons, a symbolic notation of the definition, and an illustrative case study of legislative behavior. As with most articles, however, the points the author regards as most important are contained in the introduction and conclusion. Dahl's introduction makes two points essential to understanding the later debate with his critics: first, he states his desire to capture the 'central intuitively understood meaning' of power, the 'primitive notion that seems to lie behind *all*' power concepts (e.g. influence, control, authority, etc). Toward that end he offers the idea that '*A* has power over *B* to the extent that he can get *B* to do something that *B* would not otherwise do' (Dahl 1957). The second important point in the introduction is often overlooked. It is the lament that the definition will not be 'easy to apply in concrete research problems; and therefore, [that] *operational equivalents of the formal definition, designed to meet the needs of a particular research problem, are likely to diverge from one another in important ways*' (p. 202, emphasis added).

What about the conclusion to the article? In lieu of a conventional conclusion, Dahl adopts the format of a Platonic dialog between a '"conceptual" theoretician (the protagonist) and a strict "operationalist"' (the antagonist). The conceptualizer defends the abstract definition developed earlier. The operationalist complains about a 'host of practical difficulties', such as acquiring the necessary data. The operationalist also points out that since different research problems may require different operational definitions, the idea of a single generic concept of power is useless. The conceptualizer admits that 'in practice, the concept of power will have to be defined by operational criteria that will undoubtedly modify its pure meaning'. Nevertheless, the conceptualizer argues, the generic 'concept provides us with a

ROBERT A. DAHL

standard against which to compare the operational alternatives we actually employ [and] in this way ... helps us to specify the defects of the operational definitions as measures of power'. 'To be sure', the conceptualizer concludes, 'we may have to use defective measures; but at least we shall know that they are defective and in what ways'.[4]

Thus, both the introduction and the unorthodox conclusion differentiate between the abstract generic concept of power and operational concepts of power developed for use in particular research projects. Furthermore, both the introduction and conclusion maintain that operational concepts of power are likely to diverge significantly from the abstract concept and from each other. Dahl (1961, p. 330, 1968, p. 414) reiterates these points in later publications.

The 'Community Power Debate'

The 'community power debate' is sometimes characterized as a debate between 'elitists' and 'pluralists' and at other times as a debate between sociologists and political scientists. The central issue in this debate was whether American communities were governed by a small group (the 'elite') or whether the most influential groups varied from one issue to another (the position of the 'pluralists'). Although the roots of the debate can be found in the 1950s and even in the 1930s, the debate became a major concern in political science after the publication of Dahl's (1961) study of governance in New Haven, Connecticut in 1961, entitled *Who Governs?*.

In order to determine the distribution of influence in New Haven, Dahl examined decision-making in three issue areas: (1) urban redevelopment; (2) public education; and (3) political party nominations. Those who successfully initiated policy proposals in these areas were judged to be the most influential. The overall conclusion was that the influential people in one issue area were different from those in the other issue areas – the 'pluralist' conclusion.

Since much of the subsequent criticism of *Who Governs?* refers to 'Dahl's concept of power' or to the 'pluralist concept of power', it is necessary to examine the treatment of the concept of power in this book. Surprisingly, there is no definition of the *concept* of power anywhere in *Who Governs?*. Except for the chapters on 'Indirect vs. Direct Influence' and 'Actual vs. Potential Influence', there is very little discussion of conceptual issues of any kind in the main body of the book.[5] There is, however, an appendix entitled 'Methods and Data', which contains two subsections, respectively, entitled 'The Definition and Measurement of Influence' and 'Operational Measures of Influence' (pp. 330ff). Despite its title, the first subsection offers no definition of influence, but rather advises those who wish 'to consider more rigorous formulations of the concept of influence used in this volume' to consult Dahl's 1957 article. The subsection on operational measures offers not one but six different operational definitions of influence.[6] Dahl defends the use of multiple operational definitions on the grounds that one way to 'compensate for the unsatisfactory character of all existing operational measures of influence is to be eclectic'. Expressing his desire to 'avoid putting all our eggs in one methodological basket', Dahl decides to use all six operational definitions. Thus, references to 'the concept of power in *Who Governs?*' or to the 'pluralist concept of power' may leave one wondering whether they refer to an abstract concept of power, which is

55

neither defined nor discussed in the book or to one or more of the six different operational definitions used in the analysis.

A year after the publication of *Who Governs?* Bachrach and Baratz (1962) published an article entitled 'Two Faces of Power' in the *American Political Science Review*, which criticized the book for focusing on 'the ability to initiate and veto proposals' while ignoring the ability to prevent proposals from even being considered in the first place. In essence, their argument was that influence can derive from the ability to suppress issues or to keep them off the agenda of decision-makers. This article was enormously influential and was identified as the most cited article published in the *American Political Science Review* during the 50-year period, 1945–2005 (Sigelman 2006). During the 50 years after this article was published, it was frequently depicted as having identified a defect or limitation of Dahl's concept of power (e.g. Hayward 2000, Nye 2011). This is misleading. Bachrach and Baratz were criticizing the research methodology and one of the six operational measures used in *Who Governs?*, but this criticism had little to do with the abstract concept of power underlying the book and explicated in the 1957 article. Indeed, Bachrach, and Baratz do not even cite the 1957 article. The opening sentences in their article, however, may have led some readers to expect a discussion of the *concept* of power:

> The concept of power remains elusive despite the recent and prolific outpourings of case studies on community power. Its elusiveness is dramatically demonstrated by the regularity of disagreement as to the locus of community power between the sociologists and the political scientists. (Bachrach and Baratz 1962, p. 947)

Actually, the alleged elusiveness of the concept of power had little or nothing to do with the disagreement at the center of the debate over community power. To the extent that the disagreement concerned power, it was about methodology and operational measures, not about the abstract concept of power. The concept of power explicated by Dahl in the 1957 paper is compatible with the phenomenon described by Bachrach and Baratz. Agenda control is simply one of many means by which *A* can get *B* to do something, *B* would not otherwise do.

The 'community power debate' is sometimes mischaracterized as a debate about the concept of power. Some have even described the 'discipline's discussion of power' as dating from the 1950s debate between elitists and pluralists (Valelly 2006, p. 12). The work on conceptual issues in the 1950s by Lasswell and Kaplan (1950), March (1955, 1956, 1957), Simon (1953, 1957), and Dahl (1957), however, is not concerned with the disagreements between pluralists and elitists; it is concerned with power in general. The 'power literature' and the 'community power literature' may overlap a bit, but they are not the same thing.[7] To the extent that an abstract concept lay at the heart of the community power debate, it was democracy, not power. A more accurate label for the controversy would have been 'the community democracy debate'.[8]

The 'Faces of Power'

In 1974, Steven Lukes picked up on the title of the article by Bachrach and Baratz, 'Two Faces of Power', and proposed yet a third 'face' (Lukes 1974). He described a 'one-dimensional view of power' (the first face) based on the methodology and operational definitions of influence used in *Who Governs?*, a 'two-dimensional view of power' (the second face) corresponding to the article by Bachrach and Baratz (1962), and a 'three-dimensional view of power' (the third face) that differed from the other two in the following respects: first, whereas the first two involve observable conflicts of policy preferences, the three-dimensional view allows for the possibility that A can manipulate the preferences of B so as to prevent conflict from occurring. The second difference between the three-dimensional view and the others is the assumption that the 'real interests' of B may differ from the policy preferences of B. In any case, an exercise of power is *always* detrimental to the interests of B according to the three-dimensional view. Lukes then insists that the concept of power must be defined to include 'interests' and observes that:

> the *concept* of power, thus defined, when interpreted and put to work, yields one or more *views* of power – that is, ways of identifying cases of power in the real world. The three views we have been considering can be seen as alternative interpretations and applications of one and the same underlying concept of power, according to which A exercises power over B when A affects B in a manner contrary to B's interests. (Lukes 1974, pp. 26–27)

It is important to note that Lukes differentiates between a '*concept* of power' and a '*view* of power'. Lukes' 'concept of power' is essentially the same as the concept of power explicated by Dahl in 1957 – *except*, of course, for the required detrimental effect on B's interests. What Lukes calls a 'view of power', however, is quite different. For Lukes, a 'view of power' represents a way of 'identifying cases of power in the real world' (p. 27). This corresponds with what Dahl and others call an 'operational definition', 'operational measure', and/or 'empirical indicator'. Thus, when Lukes refers to Dahl's 'view' of power as 'one-dimensional', he is not referring to the abstract concept of power explicated in 1957 (and which underlies *Who Governs?* but is not explicitly used therein), but rather to an 'operational definition' (one of six?) adopted by Dahl for purposes of a particular research project, i.e. a case study of influence in New Haven. As noted earlier, Dahl was sensitive to the difference between a concept and an operational definition adopted for use in a particular project and had warned about the likelihood of significant differences between them. Indeed, the conclusion to his 1957 article was devoted *entirely* to this issue. In 1968, Dahl went even further and warned that 'the gap between concept and operational definition is generally very great, so great, indeed, that it is not always possible to see what relation there is between the operations and the abstract definition' (Dahl 1968, p. 414).

Although Lukes is clearly aware of the difference between a concept of power and an operational definition (or 'view') of power, he expresses puzzlement when the two diverge.[9] For example, after noting that pluralist researchers often operationalize power in terms of 'actual and observable' conflict, he notes that Dahl's definition of power does not require conflict and cites passages from *Who Governs?* in which 'Dahl is quite sensitive to the operation of power or influence in the absence of conflict'. Lukes dismisses this as 'just one among a number of examples of how the text of *Who Governs?* is more subtle and profound than the general conceptual and methodological pronouncements of its author' and declares it 'in contradiction' to Dahl's 'conceptual framework' (1974, pp. 13–14). The general *conceptual* framework of *Who Governs?*, however, is drawn from Dahl's 1957 article, which is not 'in contradiction' with power in the absence of conflict. In another example, Lukes finds it 'ironic' that there are passages in the book describing the phenomenon that Lukes labels 'the three-dimensional view' (1974, p. 23). 'The trouble', Lukes asserts, 'seems to be that both Bachrach and Baratz and the pluralists suppose that because power, as they *conceptualize* it (emphasis added), only shows up in cases of actual conflict, it follows that actual conflict is necessary to power' (1974, p. 23). This assertion might be tenable if Lukes had said 'power, as they *operationalize* it', but not as it stands. These are but two of many examples of the failure by Lukes and many other critics of Dahl to distinguish between the operational definition(s) of power used in *Who Governs?* and the abstract concept of power underlying it.

It would be difficult to underestimate the influence of Lukes' treatment of the 'three faces' of power on subsequent generations of students.[10] What now passes for 'conventional wisdom' with respect to Dahl's concept of power goes something like the following:

> It is primitive, narrow, restrictive, one-dimensional, pluralist, focused on overt conflict of preferences, based on compulsion, unable to account for agenda control (second face) or control over B's wants (third face), and has been superseded by more inclusive, more sophisticated, more nuanced, concepts that yield deeper understanding.[11]

This misleading narrative cannot be attributed entirely to Lukes, since he notes that the concept of power explicated by Dahl in 1957 does not necessitate conflict and that *Who Governs?* acknowledges both agenda control and preference manipulation as instances of power (Lukes 1974, pp. 13–14). As noted above, Lukes distinguishes between Dahl's 'concept' of power and Dahl's 'view' (i.e. operational definition) of power and is careful in his use of each term. The problem is that in common parlance other people tend to use the two terms interchangeably and thereby conflate Dahl's concept of power with an operational definition of power adopted for use in a particular research project – a case study of power in New Haven. Readers may be forgiven; however, if they fail to note the difference between a 'concept' and a 'view' in Lukes' discussion, for he does not go out of his way to alert them to its importance. The distinction is mentioned only twice – once (parenthetically and in abbreviated form) in the introduction and again *after* the three 'dimensions' have been described. The only explanation of the distinction is contained in a cryptic footnote indicating that it is 'closely parallel' to a distinction by John Rawls between 'concept' and 'conception' (Lukes 1974, pp. 9, 26–27). An additional source of confusion may be that the opening sentence asserts that 'this short book presents a conceptual analysis of power'. Although there is some 'conceptual analysis' in the book, the principal focus is on describing and analyzing the three *views* of power, which are basically alternative *operational* definitions of a single underlying *concept* (1974, p. 26–27).[12] Four years after the publication of *Power: A Radical View*, Lukes (1978, p. 688) summarized the 'community power debate' as one:

> between disputants who share a general conception of asymmetric power as control ... but who disagree about how it is to be identified and measured. More specifically, they agree in seeing power as exercised when A affects B in A's but against B's interests, but they disagree about how this idea is properly to be understood and applied in research.[13]

ROBERT A. DAHL

The 'Faces of Power' revisited

In 2005, more than 30 years after the publication of *Power: A Radical View*, Lukes published a second edition, which included additional essays setting the original in historical context, clarifying its focus, and significantly revising his views with respect to the role of 'interests' in power analysis.

Context and focus

Lukes begins by describing his 1974 book as a contribution to a debate among 'American political scientists and sociologists' about 'how to think about power theoretically and how to study it empirically'. He notes that 'underlying that debate another question was at issue: how to characterize American politics – as dominated by a ruling elite or as exhibiting pluralist democracy' (2005, p. 1). He observes that:

> both methodological questions (how are we to define and investigate power?) and substantive conclusions (how pluralistic, or democratic, is its distribution?) were at issue here, as was the link between them (did the methodology predetermine the conclusions? Did it preclude others?). (2005, p. 5)

Speaking with the benefit of thirty years of hindsight, Lukes credits Dahl and his followers with having 'brought welcome and healthy precision, clarity and methodological rigour' to the study of power (2005). But he notes the 'contention of their critics … that their method was too restrictive, leading them to biased and complacent conclusions', i.e. pluralist conclusions (pp. 60–61).

In the first edition of his book, Lukes defended Dahl and others against the charge that pluralist conclusions were preordained by their 'concepts, approach, and method' (Lukes 1974, p. 11). Depending on the case at hand, their approach could yield a variety of conclusions about the distribution of power. In the second edition, Lukes describes the central focus of his 1974 book as how 'the powerful secure the compliance of those they dominate? – a narrower question than that suggested by its snappy title' (Lukes 2005, p. 110). Whereas Dahl's *Who Governs?* focused on *hypothesized* domination, Lukes' focus – as he admits in the second edition – was on *assumed* domination. There is a certain irony here, since phrasing the central question this way presupposes the existence of domination and makes pluralism definitionally impossible – precisely the sort of thing the pluralists had been unfairly accused of doing.

In 1974, Lukes had depicted his 'three-dimensional view' as 'superior to alternative views' and declared that 'the third view allows one to give a deeper and more satisfactory analysis of power relations than either of the other two' (Lukes 1974, pp. 9–10). In 2005, however, Lukes admits that the original edition was narrowly focused on why people submit to 'domination' – hardly the same question that Dahl and other pluralists were addressing. Thus, whereas Dahl's concept of power is relevant to all situations in which some people get other people to do things they would otherwise not do, Lukes' view is narrowly focused on the rare situation in which some people are 'dominating' others.[14] 'Power as domination', he now admits, 'is only one species of power' (Lukes 2005, p. 12).

ROBERT A. DAHL

Interests and power

The most important difference between Dahl's concept of power (1957) and the concept of power proposed by Lukes in 1974 was the requirement that A's power with respect to B *always* be harmful to B's interests. In the 2005 edition Lukes abandons that view, and declares 'it was a mistake' to define power that way. He admits that one 'can be powerful by satisfying and advancing others' interests', citing examples like seat belts, teaching, parenting, and 'empowering' B by increasing his resources or capabilities (2005, pp. 83–84).[15]

Lukes thus severs the conceptual link between B's interests and A's power by admitting that A's influence may be beneficial as well as harmful to B's interests. He is unwilling, however, to sever the link between A's interests and A's power. That is to say, he maintains that power is always beneficial to the interests of A. The general question of the relation between interests and power is examined by Baldwin in *Power and International Relations* (forthcoming).

Multiple and conflicting interests

In addition to the 'mistake' of insisting that power be harmful to B's interests, Lukes admits that the treatment of power in 1974 was 'inadequate' in that it assumed that actors had 'unitary interests', rather than acknowledging 'the ways in which everyone's interests are multiple, conflicting, and of different kinds' (2005, pp. 12–13). This 'inadequacy' opens up the whole idea of 'trade-offs' or 'opportunity costs' and has far-reaching implications for his discussion of Crenson's (1971) study of air pollution in Gary, Indiana. In considering why steelworkers would submit to breathing 'poison' air – presumably an instance of 'domination' harmful to their (unitary) interests – Lukes (1974, pp. 42–45) repeatedly inserted the parenthetical assumption that there were no trade-offs between unemployment and pollution. This is akin to assuming that there is, after all, such a thing as a 'free lunch'. There is, of course, a whole academic discipline built on the opposite assumption – i.e. that 'there ain't no such thing as a free lunch' (Dolan 1971).

The discipline of economics is devoted to the study of situations in which actors have multiple and competing goals (or interests), and the concept of opportunity costs is central to the discipline; yet costs (of any kind) play little or no role in either edition of Lukes' book. Oddly, Lukes notes that professional economists, 'have had little that is interesting to say about power' (2005, p. 166). He seems to have overlooked the 'interesting' contributions to the power literature by such Nobel Prize winners as John C. Harsanyi, Thomas Schelling, Herbert Simon (a political scientist), John Nash, and Lloyd Shapley, not to mention work by Oskar Morgenstern, Charles Lindblom, and Kenneth Boulding.[16]

The most puzzling – and least excusable – omission in both editions of Lukes' book is any mention of the work by Harsanyi (1962a, 1962b) on the opportunity costs of power. As noted above, the catalyst for the original book – and its principal target – was Dahl's *Who Governs?*. In an appendix subtitled 'The Definition and Measurement of Influence', Dahl goes out of his way to call attention to 'what promises to be a highly important addition to the analysis of influence' that had come to his attention 'too late to be incorporated into this study' (Dahl 1961, p. 330). He is referring to two forthcoming articles by Harsanyi on costs and power that he describes as explicitly bringing 'out what is sometimes only implicit in the present volume, the importance of opportunity costs as dimensions of power and influence'. In later works, Dahl reiterated his view of the importance of Harsanyi's contribution to the study of power (Dahl 1963, 1968, 1970).

In sum, three of the most important amendments to Lukes' 1974 pamphlet are as follows: (1) The admission of a narrow focus on a subspecies of power – domination. (2) The admission that it was a mistake to depict A's power as always detrimental to B's interests. And (3) The admission that everyone has multiple and conflicting interests. These amendments cannot be dismissed as minor tweaks to Lukes' position, and Lukes does not suggest that they should be. Those who have built their theories or analyses of power on the 1974 version of this book may want to reconsider in the light of the amendments contained in the second edition.

Dahlian power: misinterpretations

Even though Dahl writes more clearly than most social scientists, his views are often misinterpreted or mischaracterized. Since his writings on power are distributed over more than half a century, this is understandable–though unacceptable. Some, but by no means all, of these misinterpretations will be discussed below.

Concept vs. operational definition

The most common and most important misinterpretation of Dahl's concept of power stems from the failure to distinguish between abstract concepts and operational definitions.[17] As noted above, this distinction is fundamental for Dahl; and operational definitions are likely to diverge significantly not only from each other, but from the abstract concept they are designed to operationalize.[18] Thus, any attempt to infer the relevant abstract concept solely from an operational definition is problematic. Many of the misrepresentations of Dahl's concept of power discussed below are attributable to the conflation of generic and operational definitions.

The best indicator that an author is confusing concrete with abstract definitions of power is casting a discussion of Dahl's *concept* of power in terms of the 'three faces' debate.[19] As noted above, this debate revolved around different ways to operationalize the concept of power, not fundamentally different concepts. Another indicator of such confusion is an author's citations of *Who Governs?* or Lukes rather than of Dahl's general discussions of the concept of power in 1957, 1968, and various editions of *Modern Political Analysis*. Anyone seeking to understand Dahl's concept of power solely by reading *Who Governs?* is likely to be misled.

Preferences of B

Dahl's concept of power is often misconstrued to imply that A and B have conflicting desires or preferences and that a power relation must be one in which A 'wins' and B 'loses'. According to Barnett and Duvall, 'there must be a conflict of desires … A and B want different outcomes, and B loses' (Barnett and Duvall 2005 p. 49). Similarly, Nye describes Dahl's definition of power in terms of A's 'ability to get others to act in ways that are contrary to their initial preferences' (Nye 2011, pp. 11–13); and Gelb explains Dahl's concept of power in terms of A 'pressuring B to act against his will or desire' (Gelb 2009, p. 32). The preferences or wants of B, however, are *not* included in the idea of doing something B would not otherwise do. Although Dahl's phraseology for defining power evolves from 1957 to 2003, the focus is always on affecting B's behavior (including feelings, attitudes, beliefs, and predispositions to act), *not on B's wants*. Although the concept of A causing B to do something that B would not otherwise do includes getting B to act contrary to his preferences, it also includes enabling B to act in accordance with his preferences, when he otherwise would not have done so – perhaps because B lacked the knowledge, skill, motivation, or resources. Shouting 'Watch out!' to a person about to step into an open manhole is likely to cause the person to shift course, but this change in behavior is not likely to be contrary to the person's preferences or desires. Teaching B to play the piano, offering B a big reward for helping his team win a championship, providing a poor country with technical assistance that allows it to grow its own food, and using the Marshall Plan to promote European integration are all examples of influence that helps B to do something that B prefers to do.[20]

'One-dimensional' power

Lukes' characterization of Dahl's 'view' of power as 'one-dimensional' has generated a widespread perception that Dahl's 'concept' of power is narrow, restricted, and blind to the agenda control discussed by Bachrach and Baratz as well as the consciousness control described by Lukes' third dimension of power.[21] This is highly misleading. In the first place, the notion of A causing B to behave otherwise proposed by Dahl in 1957 is broad enough to include changing B's behavior by controlling agendas or suppressing issues as well as affecting B's behavior by manipulating his consciousness. In the second place, neither the methodology of *Who Governs?* nor discussions thereof are appropriate sources for understanding Dahl's abstract *concept* of power. Operational definitions adopted for use in a particular case study often diverge significantly from the abstract concept that underlies them. Therefore, it would seem advisable to base observations about Dahl's concept of power on sources in which he actually discusses the *concept* (e.g. Dahl 1957, 1963, 1968, 1970, 1976, 1984, 1991, and/or Dahl and Stinebrickner 2003). In the third place, even discussions of Dahl's concept of power based entirely on *Who Governs?* should acknowledge passages which explicitly recognize agenda control and the shaping of preferences as forms of influence (1961, pp. 161–165, 321). In the fourth place, arguments that assert or imply that Lukes broadened Dahl's concept of power rarely note that, whereas, Lukes confines the concept of power to instances in which 'A affects B in a manner contrary to B's interests' and beneficial to A's interests, Dahl's concept of power includes all instances in which A causes a change in B's behavior *regardless of the effects on the interests of either actor*. As Table 1 shows, Dahl's concept of power allows for nine possible outcomes in terms of the interests of A and B; while the concept of power proposed by Lukes in 1974 allows for only one – i.e. A wins and B loses. The concept of power proposed by Lukes in 2005, however, allows for three – i.e. those in which A wins.[22]

And in the fifth place, Dahl's concept of power has never been 'one-dimensional'. Before Lukes published his pamphlet in 1974, Dahl had explicated multiple dimensions of power, including the base, the means, the scope, the amount, the domain, the costs to A, and the costs to B. No one (with the possible exception of

ROBERT A. DAHL

Table 1. Possible outcomes of Dahlian influence.

Scenario	Actor *A*	Actor *B*
1.	Win	Win
2.	Win	Lose
3.	Lose	Win
4.	Draw	Draw
5.	Win	Draw
6.	Lose	Draw
7.	Draw	Win
8.	Draw	Lose
9.	Lose	Lose

Note: Win = Favorable to actor's interests, Lose = Unfavorable to actor's interests, Draw = Neutral with respect to actor's interests.

Lasswell and Kaplan) had done more to promote a multidimensional concept of power than Dahl. In 1970, he observed that 'power does indeed have many faces. With perseverance, one could define literally thousands of different types of influence' (Dahl 1970, p. 25). *A* footnote to this passage notes that in an appendix to the Italian translation of *Modern Political Analysis* he has shown 'how some 14,000 different types might be derived'.[23] That someone who has identified 14,000 'faces' of power should be widely regarded as having a 'one-dimensional' view of power is more than a little ironic.

Zero-sum power

The 'zero-sum concept of power' is based on the assumption that total power is limited. Consequently, any increase in one actor's power necessitates a decrease in the power of other actors in a social system. Parsons (1963a, 1963b, 1966) was the first to assert that Dahl's concept of power was an instance of zero-sum power.[24]

Neither the concept of power Dahl explicated in 1957 nor any variation described in succeeding editions of *Modern Political Analysis* embodies a zero-sum conception of power. This can be illustrated by considering the examples of Robinson Crusoe and of marriage. Although the exact wording of Dahl's concept of power has varied over a period of 50 years or so, it has always referred to situations in which one actor affects a specified aspect of the behavior of another actor. One has not defined a power relation until one has specified both scope and domain.

Thus, as long as Robinson Crusoe and Friday occupy separate islands, neither can exercise any power in the Dahlian sense. When Friday comes to live on Crusoe's island, either or both may gain power; but neither can lose what he does not have. Dahl's concept can describe this situation as one in which Crusoe and Friday each gain power over the other with respect to similar and/or different aspects of behavior (scopes). Witness the following influence attempts:

> Different scopes: 'If you will do the fishing, I will pick the fruit'. Similar scopes: 'I will do the fishing only if you fish too'.

Likewise, when two people marry, each is likely to gain power with respect to the other with respect to similar and/or different scopes:

ROBERT A. DAHL

Different scopes: 'I will do the dishes if (and only if) you will take out the garbage'. Similar scopes: I will attend the Parent-Teachers Association meeting only if you come too.

Each of these scenarios involves an increase in the influence of each actor with respect to the other, and each can be described in terms of A getting B to do x. Although Dahl's concept of power *can* describe situations in which A gains power and B loses power, it can also describe situations in which each gains power with respect to the other.[25]

James H. Read agrees that Dahl's definition of power in 1957 was not zero-sum, but suggests that it '*became* zero-sum once operationalized for purposes of research and description' (Read 2012, p. 10). According to Dahl, however, particular operational definitions of a concept, 'have to emerge from considerations of the substance and objectives of a specific piece of research, and not from general theoretical considerations'. (Dahl 1957, p. 207). Just because a concept is operationalized in zero-sum terms for a specific case study does not change the original concept.

Compulsory power

Some power analysts associate Dahl's concept of power with command, pressure, coercion, bribery, and/or compulsion. Strange (1994, p. 9), for example, declares that Dahl's concept of power 'assumes that power is exercised only by direct coercion or bribery'. Nye (2004 p. 2) cites *Who Governs?* in support of his assertion that 'some people think of power narrowly, in terms of command and coercion'. Barnett and Duvall (2005, pp. 49–50) cite Dahl's 1957 article as an example of 'compulsory power'. And Gelb interprets Dahl's concept of power as necessitating 'pressure' and excluding persuasion (2009, p. 32).

This is puzzling. Such comments give a misleading impression of Dahl's approach to analyzing power.[26] Dahl takes a very broad approach in discussing the many ways in which A can get B to do something B would not otherwise do. In 1957 (p. 203), he even mentions 'charm and charisma' as possible means for exercising power; in various editions of *Modern Political Analysis*, he discusses persuasion, rewards, friendship; and he often refers readers to Lasswell and Kaplan's (1950) forms of influence and power, which include mentorship, admiration, approbation, suasion, wisdom, love, esteem, benefaction, edification, and other forms (or bases) of power not normally associated with coercion, command, or compulsion.

Subtlety, visibility, and awareness

Nye (2011, pp. 12–16) depicts the second and third 'faces' of power as 'more subtle and therefore less visible' than Dahl's 'first face' and contends that the latter requires B to be aware of A's influence. Although there are certainly occasions when these characterizations would be accurate, they do not describe inherent qualities of the three 'faces'. North Korean leaders seem to be adept at both restricting the agendas of their citizens and at indoctrinating (or brainwashing) them into wanting to support the 'dear leader'. Their methods, however, are not particularly subtle. And Dahl's power can take very subtle forms, such as the 'charm' he

ROBERT A. DAHL

cites in 1957. It can also describe situations in which B is unaware of A's influence or even of A's existence. For example, A may get B to remove his sweater by turning up the thermostat in B's room *without B's knowledge*. Or country A may affect the behavior of country B using secret agents to mislead or sabotage country B. For example, one can imagine agents secretly inserting a computer virus into the nuclear processing facilities of another country in order to slow its progress toward producing a nuclear weapon. In sum, any of the three 'faces' of power may be subtle and invisible or crude and blatantly visible, depending on the circumstances.

Material resources

Some writers have implied that Dahl's concept of power is based on material resources. Barnett and Duvall (2005), for example, maintain that 'a widely accepted conceptualization' of power used in 'most introductory texts to international relations' is 'how one state uses its material resources to compel another state to do something it does not want to do'.(p. 40) The similarity to the wording of Dahl's classic formulation is striking.[27] Later, they suggest that this writer relies on a 'Dahlian formulation – in which A exercises influence over B' and then incorporates 'nonmaterial means of influence' (2005, p. 44). There is no need, however, to modify Dahl's concept in order to 'incorporate' nonmaterial means of influence. At no point during the last 50 years has he ever excluded 'nonmaterial means' from his concept of power.

Dahl has repeatedly cited nonmaterial means of exercising power. In 1957, he mentioned 'charm and charisma'; in 1961 and 1968, he mentioned 'popularity' and 'information'; and every edition of *Modern Political Analysis* includes references to nonmaterial power resources. The illustrative list in the fourth edition is especially instructive: money, information, food, threats of force, jobs, friendship, votes, social standing, and the right to make laws. Although it is obvious that information, friendship, votes, social standing, and the right to make laws are nonmaterial, the status of threats of force and jobs is not so obvious. Threats are signals, ideas, or understandings, which have no material existence. The same is true for jobs. A job is an arrangement between an employer and an employee; it is not something that one can taste, see, hear, feel, or smell. The rewards of a job may be material, but the job itself is not. Thus, Dahl's illustrative list of nine political resources includes at least seven nonmaterial resources. While there are those who restrict power to material resources, Dahl is certainly not one of them.

Direct and immediate

In explicating their concept of 'compulsory power' in terms of the 'direct and immediate' power of A over B, Barnett and Duvall (2005, pp. 47–50) note that power relations that are not direct and immediate are likely to be 'more difficult to observe' than those that are. 'This approach', they contend, 'is nicely summarized by Dahl's famous claim that there is "no action at a distance."' They concede that 'Dahl intentionally left vague both what counts as "distance" and the meaning of "connection"' and that his concept of power does 'not preclude the idea of power as spatially, temporally, or socially indirect or diffuse'; but, they assert, it does 'work against it.'

ROBERT A. DAHL

This is a misleading characterization of Dahl's approach to the study of power. In the first place, characterizing anyone's conceptual approach in terms that they have deliberately left 'undefined' is problematic.[28] In the second place, Dahl explains that he is leaving the concept of 'connection' undefined because he wishes 'only to call attention to the practical significance' of identifying a connection between A and B (Dahl 1957, p. 204). He is referring to a practical problem of research, not to a theoretical or conceptual problem. In the third place, the idea that power relations between A and B must be 'direct and immediate' is at odds with Dahl's views expressed elsewhere both before and after 1957. In 1953, Dahl and Lindblom identified various indirect or 'roundabout' controls such as affecting personalities, affecting social roles, and affecting agendas (Dahl and Lindblom 1953, pp. 110–112). In 1961, Dahl noted that 'indirect influence might be very great but comparatively difficult to observe and weigh. Yet to ignore indirect influence ... would be to exclude what might well prove to be a highly significant process of control' (Dahl 1961, p. 89). *Who Governs?* devoted a whole chapter to 'Direct vs. Indirect Influence', citing the influence of citizens over their elected leaders and the ability of leaders to 'shape the preferences of citizens' as examples of indirect influence (1961, pp. 163–165). In 1968, he noted that some power relationships 'are highly indirect' (1968, pp. 412–413). It should also be noted that none of the six editions of *Modern Political Analysis* describes power as direct and immediate and that the last three editions discuss several forms of indirect influence. And in the fourth place, the contention that Dahl's concept of power 'works against' the 'idea of power as spatially, temporally, or socially indirect' even though it does not preclude it is an empirical proposition unsupported by evidence. It is not even clear what 'works against' means in this context.

Conclusion

Dahl's critics have often called attention to important aspects of power relations – e.g. the suppression of issues and consciousness control. The critics, however, have not always portrayed Dahl's views as accurately as one might wish. Distinguishing between an abstract concept of power and operational definitions adopted for purposes of specific research projects is fundamental for Dahl. Furthermore, Dahl's concept of power implies nothing about the preferences of B, is not zero-sum, does not necessitate compulsion, may or may not be subtle or visible, is not confined to material resources, and may be either direct and immediate or indirect and long term.

Berenskoetter (2007, p. 2) attributes to this writer the idea that the 'three faces debate' is 'of no importance to IR' and asserts that

> for Baldwin the portrait of 'power' is not painted by theory and, therefore cannot be modified by it ... [since] abstract theoretical debates at best are repetitions on the theme and at worst obscure the true nature of power.

The point being made, however, was not that the debate has no relevance to IR, but rather that Dahl's causal concept of power could subsume all three faces. Far from viewing abstract theoretical debates as pointless, this writer's view is that the 'three faces debate' was primarily a debate about research methods, operational concepts, and democracy rather than a debate about abstract theoretical concepts of

ROBERT A. DAHL

power. Similarly, Nye (2011, p. 16) attributes to this writer the view that the three faces are 'useless abstractions'. In the first place, the three faces may be mischaracterized as 'abstractions', since they are, in Lukes' words, 'ways of identifying cases of power in the real world'. In other words, they are ways of making an abstraction (the concept of power) more concrete – and thus described more accurately as 'concretizations'. And in the second place, pointing out that the three 'views' all flow from the same abstract concept does not imply that they are 'useless abstractions'. The concept of 'writers', after all, is broad enough to subsume poets, journalists, scholars, and novelists; but it does not follow that such categories are 'useless abstractions'.

Disclosure statement

No potential conflict of interest was reported by the author.

Notes

1. See, for example, Gruber (2000), Hayward (2000), Morriss (2002), Barnett and Duvall (2005), Berenskoetter and Williams (2007), Gallarotti (2010), Finnemore and Goldstein (2013), Guzzini (2013).
2. Following Dahl's usage in 1957, the terms power and influence will be used interchangeably here.
3. Describing the community power debate as one between Dahl and his critics can be misleading, since Dahl is more accurately described as a target for his critics than as an active participant in the debate. Shortly before his retirement, he observed that he had not wanted to spend his time 'answering critics' and mused that he may have 'done less of that than [he was] properly obliged to do' (Baer *et al.* 1991, p. 176). Dahl's reluctance to engage his critics may account for some of the later misinterpretations of his concept of power.
4. Most of Dahl's critics make no reference to the 'conclusion' of this article. Stewart R. Clegg is an exception. He portrays the conceptualizer ('a nit-picking sort of character') as the antagonist and the operationalist (with whom 'we are clearly led to sympathize') as the protagonist (1989, p. 54).The title of the article, the thrust of the argument, and the fact that Dahl gives the first and last word to the conceptualizer would seem to argue against Clegg's interpretation.
5. For example, even though the ability to 'initiate' successful policy proposals plays an important part in the analysis, the concept of initiation is ignored. For a discussion of the *concept* of initiation, see Baldwin (1966).
6. The terms operational definition and operational measure are often used interchangeably.
7. An influential collection of articles on power published between 1950 and 1968 contained 27 entries, of which only 5 focused on the 'community power' debate (Bell *et al.* 1969).
8. For an overview of the 'community power debate', see Ricci (1980). This article hardly mentions abstract concepts of power, but focuses instead on methodology and democracy. See also Polsby (1980).
9. Whether Lukes was familiar with Dahl's 1968 article on 'Power' is problematic. He neither cites it nor includes it in the bibliography of the 1974 edition. Nor does he consider either of the first two editions of *Modern Political Analysis*.
10. A Google Scholar search reveals more than twice as many citations to Lukes' book as to Dahl's 1957 article – about the same number as citations for Dahl's article and *Who Governs?* combined.
11. While no single author subscribes to all of the elements of this dominant narrative, the following provide examples of various combinations of its elements: Clegg (1989),

ROBERT A. DAHL

Strange (1994), Gruber (2000), Hayward (2000), Barnett and Duvall (2005), Berenskoetter (2007), Grewal (2008), Nye (2011), Finnemore and Goldstein (2013).

12. In his annotated bibliography Lukes dismisses Dahl's 'Concept of Power' as a 'first, rather crude effort to define and operationalise "power"'. He praises *Who Governs?* as 'a finer, subtler work than its critics and defenders might suggest, partly because it contains the evidential basis for criticizing its conclusions'. (1974, p. 60).

13. On the question of whether power should be considered as 'asymmetric', see Baldwin (1978).

14. 'Domination' is perhaps the most abused and ill-defined term in the lexicon of power.

15. Any parent of a two-year-old or a rebellious teenager, of course, could have identified this defect in Lukes' 1974 definition of power. Of course, there are also times when 'disempowering' a two-year-old by decreasing his resources is in his interest – e.g. 'you can't play with that gun, hammer, or knife'. Likewise, it may be in the interest of a teenager to 'disempower' him or her by taking away the car keys.

16. In the second edition, Lukes does mention Boulding's (1989) book as a 'thoughtful' book.

17. On the importance of drawing a 'clear distinction between measurement issues and disputes about concepts', see Adcock and Collier (2001).

18. The divergence between operational concepts and the abstract concept they are intended to operationalize is not unique to Dahl's concept of power. King *et al.* (1994) make a similar point. Barnett and Duvall (2005, p. 40) contend that 'there is a widely accepted conceptualization [of power] that is viewed as the only way to understand power: how one state uses its material resources to compel another state to do something it does not want to do'. They add that 'attempts by scholars to operationalize power follow from this definition'. Actually, a wide variety of operational definitions could 'follow from' this definition, depending on the specific research project at hand.

19. Examples abound, but see Clegg (1989), Hayward (2000), Berenskoetter (2007), Grewal (2008), and Nye (2011). A particularly influential – and misleading – example is Gaventa (1980, 2007), who quotes Dahl's 1957 'intuitive idea of power' and immediately follows it with a quote from Polsby (1980) to the effect that community power may be studied by examining 'who participates, who gains and who loses, and who prevails in decision-making'. Gaventa neglects to point out that Polsby is identifying only one of many different ways to operationalize Dahl's abstract concept of power, thus leaving the reader with the impression that there is some necessary connection between the two. Contrary to this impression, Dahl's abstract concept of power implies nothing about participation, who gains, who loses, or who prevails in decision-making.

20. The Marshall Plan example is solely for illustrative purposes. I should like to sidestep the question of whether European countries really preferred integration.

21. As noted above, Lukes himself is careful to distinguish between Dahl's 'concept' of power and what Lukes labels Dahl's 'view' of power. His readers, however, often overlook this distinction. Dahl's concept of power is depicted as narrow and one-dimensional by Nye (2004, 2011), Gruber (2000), Hayward (2000), Barnett and Duvall (2005), Grewal (2008), Gaventa (1980, 2007), Berenskoetter (2007), and countless others. Oddly, Berenskoetter attributes Dahl's definition of '*A* getting *B* to do something *B* would otherwise not do' to *Who Governs?* and to Dahl's article in the *International Encyclopedia of the Social Sciences* even though it appears in neither.

22. Any given instance of *A*'s influence with respect to *B* may have both favorable and unfavorable effects on the interests of either actor. Thus, winning, losing, and drawing are here defined in terms of their *net* impact on the interests of each actor.

23. Dahl also described the process for calculating the 14,000 'faces' in a paper delivered at the 1964 annual meeting of the American Political Association and reprinted in Dahl (1997, pp. 295–296).

24. Parsons also attributed a zero-sum concept of power to C. Wright Mills, V. O. Key, and to Lasswell and Kaplan. For a discussion of whether this applied to Lasswell and Kaplan, see Baldwin (1989). Others who have designated Dahl's concept of power as zero-sum include Scott (2001), Barnett and Duvall (2005), Berenskoetter (2007), and Dowding (2012). The attribution of a zero-sum concept of power to Dahl is usually asserted without explanation of the basis for the assertion, as if it were self-evident.

ROBERT A. DAHL

25. There are only three possible outcomes to a zero-sum game (win, lose, draw). As Table 1 shows, however, Dahl's concept of power allows for nine possible outcomes.
26. Early on, Dahl often used the terms power and influence interchangeably. In later editions of *Modern Political Analysis*, he adopts the language of Lasswell and Kaplan in treating 'power' as a subtype of 'influence'. This is more of a terminological change than a conceptual one. This change of terminology, however, does not explain the comments above, since they rely on the 1957 article and on *Who Governs?*
27. This assertion about 'most texts' is not supported by references to specific texts.
28. Hayward (2000, p. 36) goes further than Barnett and Duvall in describing Dahl's comment about 'no action at a distance' as 'explicit and uncompromising'. When terms are explicitly left undefined, however, phrases like 'implicit and wishy-washy' would seem to be more apt descriptions.

References

Adcock, R. and Collier, D., 2001. Measurement validity: a shared standard for qualitative and quantitative research. *American Political Science Review*, 95 (3), 529–546.

Bachrach, P. and Baratz, M.S., 1962. Two faces of power. *American Political Science Review*, 56 (4), 947–952.

Baer, M.A., Jewell, M., and Sigelman, L., eds., 1991. *Political science in America: oral histories of a discipline*. Lexington, KY: University Press of Kentucky.

Baldwin, D.A., 1966. Congressional initiative in foreign policy. *Journal of Politics*, 28 (4), 754–773.

Baldwin, D.A., 1978. Power and social exchange. *American Political Science Review*, 72 (4), 1229–1242.

Baldwin, D.A., 1989. *Paradoxes of power*. New York: Basil Blackwell.

Baldwin, D.A., Forthcoming. *Power and international relations*. Princeton, NJ: Princeton University Press.

Barnett, M. and Duvall, R., 2005. Power in international politics. *International Organization*, 59 (1), 39–75.

Bell, R., Edwards, D.V., and Wagner, H.R., eds., 1969. *Political power: a reader in theory and research*. New York: Free Press.

Berenskoetter, F., 2007. Thinking about power. *In*: F. Berenskoetter and M.J. Williams, eds. *Power in world politics*. London: Routledge, 1–22.

Berenskoetter, F. and Williams, M.J., eds., 2007. *Power in world politics*. London: Routledge.

Boulding, K.E., 1989. *Three faces of power*. London: Sage.

Clegg, S.R., 1989. *Frameworks of power*. London: Sage.

Crenson, M., 1971. *The un-politics of air pollution: a study of non-decisionmaking in the cities*. Baltimore, MD: Johns Hopkins University Press.

Dahl, R.A., 1957. The concept of power. *Behavioral Science*, 2 (3), 201–215.

Dahl, R.A., 1961. *Who governs?* New Haven, CT: Yale University Press.

Dahl, R.A., 1963. *Modern political analysis*. Englewood Cliffs, NJ: Prentice-Hall.

Dahl, R.A., 1968. Power. *International encyclopedia of the social sciences*. New York: Free Press, 405–415.

Dahl, R.A., 1970. *Modern political analysis*. Englewood Cliffs, NJ: Prentice-Hall.

Dahl, R.A., 1976. *Modern political analysis*. Englewood Cliffs, NJ: Prentice-Hall.

Dahl, R.A., 1984. *Modern political analysis*. Englewood Cliffs, NJ: Prentice-Hall.

Dahl, R.A., 1991. *Modern political analysis*. Englewood Cliffs, NJ: Prentice-Hall.

ROBERT A. DAHL

Dahl, R.A., 1997. *Toward democracy: a journey, reflections 1940–1997*. Berkeley, CA: Institute of Governmental Studies, University of California, Berkeley.

Dahl, R.A. and Lindblom, C.E., 1953. *Politics, economics, and welfare: planning and politico-economic systems resolved into basic social processes*. New York: Harper & Row.

Dahl, R.A. and Stinebrickner, B., 2003. *Modern political analysis*. Upper Saddle River, NJ: Prentice-Hall.

Dolan, E.G., 1971. *TANSTAAFL: a libertarian perspective on environmental policy*. New York: Holt, Rinehart, and Winston.

Dowding, K., 2012. Why should we care about the definition of power? *Journal of Political Power*, 5 (1), 119–135.

Finnemore, M. and Goldstein, J., eds., 2013. *Back to basics: state power in a contemporary world*. New York: Oxford University Press.

Gallarotti, G.M., 2010. *Cosmopolitan power in international relations*. Cambridge: Cambridge University Press.

Gaventa, J., 1980. *Power and powerlessness*. Chicago, IL: University of Chicago Press.

Gaventa, J., 2007. Levels, spaces and forms of power. *In*: F. Berenskoetter and M.J. Williams, eds. *Power in world politics*. London: Routledge, 204–224.

Gelb, L., 2009. *Power rules*. New York: Harper Collins.

Grewal, D.S., 2008. *Network power*. New Haven, CT: Yale University Press.

Gruber, L., 2000. *Ruling the world*. Princeton, NJ: Princeton University Press.

Guzzini, S., 2013. *Power, realism, and constructivism*. London: Routledge.

Harsanyi, J.C., 1962a. Measurement of social power in n-person reciprocal power situations. *Behavioral Science*, 7 (1), 81–91.

Harsanyi, J.C., 1962b. Measurement of social power, opportunity costs, and the theory of two-person bargaining games. *Behavioral Science*, 7 (1), 67–80.

Hayward, C.R., 2000. *De-facing power*. Cambridge: Cambridge University Press.

King, G., Keohane, R.O., and Verba, S., 1994. *Designing social inquiry*. Princeton, NJ: Princeton University Press.

Lasswell, H.D. and Kaplan, A., 1950. *Power and society: a framework for political inquiry*. New Haven, CT: Yale University Press.

Lukes, S., 1974. *Power: a radical view*. London: Macmillan.

Lukes, S., 1978. Power and authority. *In*: T. Bottomore and R. Nisbet, eds. *A history of sociological analysis*. New York: Basic Books, 633–676.

Lukes, S., 2005. *Power: a radical view*. 2nd ed. New York: Palgrave Macmillan.

March, J.G., 1955. An introduction to the theory and measurement of influence. *American Political Science Review*, 49 (2), 431–451.

March, J.G., 1956. Influence measurement in experimental and semi-experimental groups. *Sociometry*, 19 (4), 260–271.

March, J.G., 1957. Measurement concepts in the theory of influence. *Journal of Politics*, 19 (2), 202–226.

Morriss, P., 2002. *Power: a philosophical analysis*. 2nd ed. Manchester: Manchester University Press.

Nye, J.S., 2004. *Soft power: the means to success in world politics*. New York: Public Affairs.

Nye, J.S., 2011. *The future of power*. New York: Public Affairs.

Parsons, T., 1963a. On the concept of influence. *Public Opinion Quarterly*, 27 (1), 37–62.

Parsons, T., 1963b. On the concept of political power. *Proceedings of the American Philosophical Society*, 107, 232–262.

Parsons, T., 1966. The political aspect of social structure and process. *In*: D. Easton, ed. *Varieties of political theory*. Englewood Cliffs, NJ: Prentice-Hall, 71–112.

Pettit, P., 2008. Dahl's power and republican freedom. *Journal of Power*, 1 (1), 67–74.

Polsby, N.W., 1980. *Community power and political theory*. New Haven, CT: Yale University Press.

Rae, D.W., 1988. Knowing power: a working paper. *In*: I. Shapiro and G. Reeher, eds. *Power, inequality, and democratic politics: essays in honor of Robert A. Dahl*. London: Westview Press, 17–49.

Read, J.H., 2012. Is power zero-sum or variable-sum? Old arguments and new beginnings. *Journal of Political Power*, 5 (1), 5–31.

Ricci, D., 1980. Receiving ideas in political analysis: the case of community power studies, 1950–1970. *Western Political Quarterly*, 33 (4), 451–475.

Scott, J., 2001. *Power*. Cambridge: Polity Press.

Sigelman, L., 2006. American political science review citation classics. *American Political Science Review*, 100 (4), 667–669.

Simon, H., 1953. Notes on the observation and measurement of political power. *Journal of Politics*, 15 (4), 500–516.

Simon, H., 1957. *Models of man*. New York: Wiley.

Strange, S., 1994. Who governs? Networks of power in world society. *Hitotsubashi Journal of Law and Politics*, 22 (Special Issue), 5–17.

Valelly, R.M., 2006. Power reconsidered, *Presented at the 102nd Annual Meeting of American Political Science Association*, 31 August–3 September 2006 Philadelphis, PA.

Dahl's concept of leadership: notes towards a theory of leadership in a democracy

Nannerl O. Keohane

School of Social Science, Institute for Advanced Study, Einstein Drive, Princeton, USA

Robert Dahl's writings contain a number of intriguing passages about leadership. The relevant sections appear in several of his key writings, including the *Preface to Democratic Theory*, *Who Governs?*, *Modern Political Analysis*, *After the Revolution,* and *Democracy and its Critics*. In these works, Dahl's conception of leadership evolves from an emphasis on 'control' to 'influence', and finally broadens to include 'competence' and 'expertise'. These sections are episodic and disconnected from one work to another; they repay close attention, nonetheless. This essay identifies these promising themes and sketches out some directions that a political theory of democratic leadership based on Dahl's insights might take.

Democracy and leadership

Robert Dahl was one of the paradigmatic theorists of democracy, not only for the late twentieth century, but for all time. His books and articles about democracy span five decades, from *A Preface to Democratic Theory* in 1956 to *On Political Equality* (2006). These works shed light on participatory and representative democracy, constitutional systems and pluralism, urban politics, governance in non-state organizations such as trade unions, corporations or the PTA, and the concept of global democracy. The term he coined for a democratic government in a large complex society – 'polyarchy' – has entered the lexicon of political science.

Throughout his career, Dahl focused primarily on the role of citizens in democratic governments. With notable consistency, he highlighted the same ideal requirements for citizenship in a democracy: final control over the political agenda by the citizens, regular opportunities to elect or reject their representatives, unconstrained access to information, and relative political equality.

Most students of politics would also associate Dahl's name with the concept of 'power'. However, with the notable exception of *Who Governs?,* it is unlikely that many would think of him in connection with the analysis of 'leadership'. Yet Dahl's theoretical writings include a number of intriguing passages about citizens as leaders. The passages that discuss leadership are episodic, disconnected from one work to another. They repay close attention, nonetheless, and provide a set of suggestions for a theory of leadership in democratic systems. The purpose of this essay is to identify these promising themes, and thus lay the groundwork for a more comprehensive account of leadership in a democracy.

ROBERT A. DAHL

In this discussion, I will rely on the definition of leadership I used in *Thinking about Leadership*: 'Leaders determine or clarify goals for a group of individuals and bring together the energies of members of that group to accomplish those goals' (Keohane 2010, p. 23, italics added).

Leadership is a distinctive dimension of human social relationships. It is not reducible to power, rule, or authority, although it has a close kinship with each of these concepts and often overlaps with them. Almost all leaders exercise some degree of power, but not all individuals who wield power are leaders. Think of a playground bully or a mugger with a gun. Many leaders are in positions of authority, but much leadership occurs in unofficial contexts where the individuals who lead have no formal authority. And quite a few individuals in authority are not providing anything that counts as leadership. As John Gardner puts it, 'We have all occasionally encountered top persons who couldn't lead a squad of seven-year-olds to the ice cream counter' (Gardner 1990, p. 2).

Leadership in this sense – clarifying goals and mobilizing energies – is essential to all social action of any degree of complexity. Leadership in a democracy presents specific challenges and opportunities compared with leadership in an autocratic system. Yet democracies cannot function without leadership, any more than any other political arrangement. *Attention to only one side of the leadership/citizenship symbiosis that makes up democratic governance cannot give us a fully rounded picture of the workings of this kind of political system.*

In Dahl's earliest theoretical writings, leaders of a democracy are considered primarily as objects for *control* by the citizens as a whole. *Who Governs?* (1961) marks a turning point in his work. From that point forward, he discusses leadership in a democratic polity by identifying persons of unusual *influence* compared to other citizens. There are shrewd discussions of bargaining among elites and the particular advantages enjoyed by those who possess and use unusually large portfolios of political resources. These passages demonstrate a sure sense of the importance of access to political resources and their skillful use for effective action in any political system. However, leaders are rarely depicted as political entrepreneurs, and never as inspiring figures. Dahl's approach fails to encompass the Nelson Mandelas or Franklin D. Roosevelts, and gives only limited scope to more typical mayors, governors, or presidents.

Dahl's asymmetrical analysis of democracy is particularly unfortunate because of his exceptional influence on many other democratic theorists. However, Dahl is hardly alone in this asymmetry. With a few exceptions (Jean-Jacques Rousseau and J.S. Mill among them), democratic theorists from Aristotle to the present day have paid little attention to the potential positive contributions of leaders in a democratic political system. This neglect has resulted in a significant lacuna in our understanding of how democracies work. *Both leaders and those who elect them are crucial parts of the symbiosis that makes up a democratic polity.* As Rousseau pointed out, a 'people' (or in Dahl's sense, a *demos*) cannot act on its own; it needs leaders who can create effective institutions, respond to expressions of popular will, take initiative, and implement decisions. (Rousseau 1997 [1762], p. 68; book II: 6).

This essay is organized chronologically. I begin with the concept of leadership in *Politics, Economics and Welfare* (written with Charles A. Lindblom in 1953) and in Dahl's first major theoretical works, the *Preface to Democratic Theory* (1956) and 'The Concept of Power' (1957). In all these writings, Dahl treats power in terms of control. Next we look at *Who Governs?* (1961), a crucial text in which

ROBERT A. DAHL

Dahl analyzes the goals and behavior of actual leaders in a democratic system. The dominant theme is leadership as 'influence', and the ways in which influence is acquired and used. Dahl's subsequent theoretical writings rely on this concept.

I turn then to the discussions of leadership in the theoretical writings from *Modern Political Analysis* (1963) through *On Polyarchy* (1971). I argue that Dahl's thought-provoking book *After the Revolution* (1970) includes some particularly interesting insights. I explore the analysis of 'guardianship' in *Democracy and its Critics* (1989). In a brief conclusion, I bring together several of the themes I have identified and consider what they might teach us about leadership.

Delegation and control

Dahl and Lindblom's *Politics, Economics and Welfare* discusses 'rational social action' in terms of both calculation and control. The authors note that when individuals delegate choices to others, they 'reduce the number of variables' they need to understand and manage. One significant instance is that 'in many social organizations individuals delegate choices to leaders' (Dahl and Lindblom 1953, p. 71).

'In many situations', the authors go on to say, 'optimum rationality would be impossible without leaders to whom choices can be delegated'. The definition of leadership provided here: 'leaders are those who have significantly greater control over decisions than other members of a group'. Non-leaders may lack both the knowledge and expertise to make good decisions, or may not wish to expend the time and take on the responsibility for making those decisions. And 'in some cases individuals do not know what they want and yet are reasonably sure that they do not want what they have now'. In such situations, leadership is particularly valuable.

Dahl and Lindblom explicitly reject the 'Benthamite view that no one can know his own wants better than the individual himself'. In some instances, those with more expertise may be able to figure out what I 'really' want better than I can myself. (Dahl and Lindblom, p. 72) The example given here is the BBC in Great Britain, explicitly charged by democratically elected governments 'to change the aesthetic and intellectual level of its listeners, not solely to cater to it'. This striking claim that someone else might occasionally have a better sense of my own wants or needs than I have has enormous implications for any theory of democracy. The statement is left orphaned in this discussion, never developed in any greater depth. However, Dahl returns to this general concept later in his career by exploring the concept of 'guardianship'.

One of the most interesting sections of *Politics, Economics and Welfare* is the discussion of 'hierarchy', control *by* leaders (including officials in a bureaucracy), juxtaposed to the section that follows, on 'polyarchy', which treats the control *of* leaders by citizens. In this context, the authors develop more fully their 'operational definition' of leadership. 'A good first approximation is to say that if individuals in a group were ranked according to the "extent" of their control over one another, the leader or leaders would be those with "significantly" greater control' (Dahl and Lindblom, p. 228).

Dahl and Lindblom define control as follows: 'B is controlled by A to the extent that B's responses are dependent in A's acts in an immediate and direct functional way'. The book explores a number of types of control in human relationships, including those that involve force and the more common form that operates through 'the subjective field' of an individual (Dahl and Lindblom, p. 94, 95). The concept of 'control' plays a complex and somewhat confusing role in this discussion. Voters 'control' leaders, even as they delegate choices to them. And leaders, in turn, 'control' decisions made within the group. Leaders also 'control' citizens and other leaders through the layers of a bureaucracy. Given the highly abstract tone of the argument, there is little helpful insight into how these complex relationships between leaders and other citizens actually work.

Defining leadership in terms of delegation and control captures two relevant facets of what leadership means in a government based on popular sovereignty. But these definitions ignore the central work of leadership: political entrepreneurs acting to clarify goals and mobilize the energies of people to pursue those goals – and the leader's goals as well.

In one brief section of the book, Dahl and Lindblom do recognize this important dimension of leadership. The authors assert 'among two or three individuals, no doubt the leader is commonly the one who most frequently initiates the actions taken by the group'. In large groups, leaders are unlikely 'to initiate actions *directly*'. Instead, leaders 'veto, endorse, modify, postpone, and pigeon-hole actions or proposed actions initiated by others. Nevertheless – and this is vital', they continue, 'the leader is in a strategic position to initiate actions when he feels they are needed'. Thus 'the *strategic opportunity* of the leader to initiate actions when he wishes to do so is one of his most important characteristics' (Dahl and Lindblom, p. 230, italics in the original).

A Preface to Democratic Theory also focuses on 'control' as the central factor in political analysis. 'At a minimum', says Dahl, 'democratic theory is concerned with processes by which ordinary citizens exert a relatively high degree of control over leaders' (Dahl 1956, p. 3). The analysis in *Preface* builds on this conception of 'control' of leaders by followers, attending primarily to the most effective ways to ensure responsiveness to the preferences of citizens.

The discussion of the conditions under which citizens may effectively control their leaders – the form of government he calls 'polyarchy' – is breathtakingly idealistic, which Dahl recognizes. He notes that 'it may be laid down dogmatically that no human organization – certainly none with more than a handful of people – has ever met or is ever likely to meet these eight conditions' (Dahl 1956, p. 71). Yet as the discussion proceeds, he brings in several more realistic points, including variations among citizens in skill, participation, and socioeconomic status. He notes 'that the number of individuals who exercise significant control over the alternatives scheduled is, in most organizations, only a tiny fraction of the total membership'.

Anyone attentive to the importance of leadership in a democracy would pause here to ask: Who are these individuals? How do they get into a position where they can exercise such control, and what do they do with this power? In the *Preface,* Dahl is unconcerned with such questions.

In his well-known essay on 'The Concept of Power', published shortly after the *Preface*, Dahl clarifies the concept of power for operational purposes. A whole cluster of words connects to the idea of power, including influence, control, authority, and rule. Some degree of slippage among these words does not bother him because he sees them all as closely related. 'In this essay', Dahl claims, 'I am seeking to explicate the primitive notion that seems to lie behind *all* of these concepts.

ROBERT A. DAHL

Some of my readers would doubtless prefer the term "influence," while others may insist that I am talking about "control"'. He asks to 'be permitted to use these terms interchangeably when it is convenient to do so' (Dahl 1957, p. 202).

This is a striking statement, given that for many English speakers, there is a significant distinction between 'influencing' someone and 'controlling' them. When I 'influence' something or someone, someone else may also be bringing influence to bear in the same situation. If I 'control' someone or something, the relationship is exclusive and determinative. Later in his work, Dahl himself recognized that the two concepts do not overlap completely. However, the elision between these two terms at this stage of his thinking is important for our purposes because, as I discuss in the next section, Dahl's analysis of power now shifts from an emphasis on 'control' to one of 'influence'. Given his discussion in 'The Concept of Power', it appears that for Dahl, this transition was almost seamless.

Dahl defines power in these terms: 'My intuitive idea of power', he tells us, 'is something like this: A has power over B to the extent that he can get B to do something that B would not otherwise do'. In spelling out this definition, he insists that 'power is a relation, and that it is a relation among people', which for this purpose means a varied group of actors including 'individuals, groups, roles, offices, governments, nation-states and other human aggregates' (Dahl 1957, p. 203).

Dahl's point that power is a *relationship* is particularly important. In earlier discussions by social scientists, power was often a mysterious *attribute* possessed in greater or lesser degree by different people or different states. Defining power as a relationship rather than an attribute is a step forward for several reasons. This definition allows us to focus on the resources that actors may use, and it is context-specific. Whether a particular resource makes it possible to influence others, or control decisions, depends on the situation (Baldwin 1979).

Dahl's definition of power is vigorous, straightforward, and active. It puts the emphasis squarely on the intentions and effectiveness of actor A. This definition launched a fruitful debate on the meaning of 'power' that continues to the present day.

Who governs? Influence and the ambiguity of leadership

The theoretical abstraction that characterizes Dahl's early work gives way to a close focus upon actual leaders and their activities when Dahl turns, a few years later, to the political system of New Haven, CT. The opening sentence of *Who Governs?* directs us immediately to the issue of leadership as rule or governance: 'In a political system where nearly every adult may vote but where knowledge, wealth, social position, access to officials, and other resources are unequally distributed, who actually governs?' (Dahl 1961, p. 1).

Dahl notes that several familiar community power studies claim that 'beneath the façade of democratic politics a social and economic elite will usually be found to be actually running things'. This hypothesis 'left very little room for the politician. He was usually regarded merely as an agent – of majority will, the political parties, interests groups, or the elite. He had no independent influence' (Dahl 1961, p. 6). In this connection, Dahl mentions Machiavelli's description of a 'cunning, resourceful, masterful leader', who 'knows how to use his resources to the maximum' and is thus 'not so much the agent of others as others are his agents'.

ROBERT A. DAHL

Dahl's own definition of leadership at this point emphasizes *influence*: leaders are 'the most influential people' in the community (Dahl 1961, p. 7). The identification of leadership in a democracy with a pattern of unequal resources is a theme that runs through Dahl's work from this time forward. Having done extensive field research in his city, Dahl sees leaders no longer as merely objects of control, as in the *Preface*; yet neither are they independent Machiavellian political entrepreneurs. Instead, they occupy a middling status: they have political resources that they bring to bear effectively and thus have more *influence* than other citizens in political activity.

To understand Dahl's analysis here, it is helpful to refer to a later discussion in *Dilemmas of Pluralist Democracy* of *power, influence* and *control*. 'Attempts to clarify the meaning of terms like *power, influence,* and *control* have produced an over abundance of names and definitions', Dahl claims. To bring order to this motley collection of concepts, he distinguishes both control and power from the provision of 'benefits' (Dahl 1982, p. 17). Departing from his earlier willingness to conflate control and influence, he notes here that 'control is also both more inclusive and less inclusive than certain other concepts'. Yet at the same time, 'control is narrower than influence, at least in the broad meaning of influence' (Dahl 1982, p. 18). If I control someone or something, it is necessarily true that I influence that person or entity. But I may *influence* someone or something and not control the object of my influence.

In *Who Governs?*, Dahl defines influence as follows: 'A rough test of a person's overt or covert influence is the frequency with which he successfully *initiates an important policy* over the opposition of others, or vetoes policies initiated by others, or initiates policy where no opposition appears' (Dahl 1961, p. 66). Influence here becomes the ability to *take independent action* to move effectively against opposition or stagnation. Given that Dahl in 'The Concept of Power' has defined power as a 'relationship', it is striking that in this context of policy initiation, the relationship is immediately one of competition or combat, rather than collaboration or compromise. A concept of collective power such as Hannah Arendt's has no place in Dahl's political universe (Arendt 1958, p. 200–202).

Chapter 8 of *Who Governs*, entitled 'The Ambiguity of Leadership', is one of the most sustained and perceptive discussions of leadership in Dahl's writings. The 'ambiguity' here has to do with the distinctive relationship between leaders and citizens. 'Viewed from one position, leaders are enormously influential', and might even be taken to be a kind of 'ruling elite'. However, viewed from a different perspective, 'Many influential leaders seem to be captives of their constituents' (Dahl 1961, p. 89).

In this chapter, Dahl makes a number of important points about the ambiguity of leadership in a democracy.

First, in order to gain legitimacy for their actions, leaders in the American context 'frequently surround their covert behavior with democratic rituals'. This makes their activities more palatable to other citizens; it also makes it harder to figure out what they are actually doing. This observation is echoed by thoughtful leaders reflecting on their own political experience. Describing his introduction to electoral politics in *Fire and Ashes*, Michael Ignatieff tells us how he had to learn how to give answers to questions asked by voters that paid due attention to their expectations and needs. References to his own ambitions or his hopes to learn useful things from serving in office were not likely to be acceptable; he needed to focus on what he could do for those who elected him. 'These circumlocutions are the

ROBERT A. DAHL

etiquette of democracy, the ritual salute to the sovereignty of the people', he says. 'Such dissembling may have its uses', he continues. 'The pretense may begin as a piece of hypocrisy and end up becoming a politician's second nature' (Ignatieff 2013, p. 7, 8).

Second, Dahl argues that among all those who influence a decision, 'some do so more directly than others', in the sense that they are 'closer to the stage where concrete alternatives' are discussed and decided. It would be wrong, however, to ignore 'indirect influence' in this process as well.

Third, the relationship between leaders and citizens in a pluralistic democracy is frequently reciprocal. Leaders influence decisions made by constituents, but the decisions of leaders are also 'determined in part' by what they believe to be the preferences of their constituents.

For all these reasons, leadership in a democracy is symbiotic, occluded, and highly ambiguous, and it is often unwise to take the behavior you may observe at face value.

Dahl concludes that

> in any durable association of more than a handful of individuals', a relatively small proportion 'exercises a relatively great direct influence over all the important choices bearing on the life of the association. (Dahl 1961, p. 95)

These persons, he says, 'are, by definition, the leaders'. As we have seen, in the *Preface,* he offered this observation as a general truth about politics. In *Who Governs?,* he demonstrates how this actually works. Leaders are motivated by many different kinds of goals and motives, and rely on many different strategies to achieve them.

To achieve these goals, 'auxiliaries or subleaders are needed'. In order to secure their services, these individuals must be rewarded with either financial or non-financial pay-offs. The success of leaders also depends on the views of constituents, who tend to have rather different sets of goals from the subleaders, and require different kinds of rewards. The tension between these two necessary strategies of leadership – satisfying both the subleaders and the constituents – is one of the most important energizing factors in a democratic polity like New Haven.

Here again, Dahl's account is supported by politicians who have spent time in the trenches.

> The gulf between representatives and the people cannot be fully overcome. You and your voters do not share the same information, the same space, or the same concerns. Political issues divide roughly into two: those that matter only to politicians and to the tiny in-group of press and partisans who follow the game, and the much smaller number that matter to the people at large. (Ignatieff 2013, p. 102)

Dahl brings all of this together in concluding the chapter on the ambiguity of leadership with these words:

> To be sure, in a pluralistic system with dispersed inequalities, the direct influence of leaders on policies extends well beyond the norms implied in the classical models of democracy developed by political philosophers. But if the leaders lead, they are also led. Thus the relations between leaders, subleaders, and constituents produce in the distribution of influence a stubborn and pervasive ambiguity that permeates the entire political system. (Dahl 1961, p. 101, 102)

ROBERT A. DAHL

After completing *Who Governs?,* Dahl returned to the more abstract analytical mode that had characterized his earlier writings. He never attempted another real-world field study of this kind, but what he learned in exploring the politics of New Haven had significant implications for the development of his theory in later years.

Leadership as influence

In *Modern Political Analysis,* Dahl notes that 'the most obvious political roles are played by persons who create, interpret and enforce rules that are binding on members of a political system' (Dahl 1963, p. 11). In a markedly Aristotelian vein, he asserts that 'these roles are "offices," and the collection of offices in a political system is what constitutes the government of that system' (Aristotle 1962, p. 110; 1278b) Although the word 'leader' does not appear in this passage, the central place Dahl gives to the official roles occupied by those citizens who are (temporarily) in positions of authority in a democracy is important for his concept of political leadership.

In discussing the processes that characterize the workings of any political system, Dahl gives particular emphasis to 'political resources' and their use. He defines a 'political resource' as 'a means by which one person can influence the behavior of other persons', including 'money, information, food, the threat of force, jobs, friendship, social standing, the right to make laws, votes, and a great variety of other things'. Then he lists 'four reasons why control over political resources is unevenly distributed in virtually all societies' (Dahl 1963, p. 15).

The first factor is the 'specialization of function' that necessarily exists in any human society, which 'creates differences in access to different political resources' (Dahl 1963, p. 15). Political officers have more access to information, and often more opportunity to use the threat of force, than other citizens. Uneven access to political resources is also explained by variations in 'endowments', both biological and social, which 'produce differences in the incentives and goals of different people in a society'. This unevenness in political resources might seem to threaten the equality among citizens that Dahl has described as a hallmark of democracy. Yet 'some differences in incentives and goals are usually regarded as socially beneficial because it is necessary to equip individuals for different specialities' if a complex human society is to work.

Against this background, Dahl uses the approach he developed in *Who Governs?* to describe leadership in terms of 'influence'. He observes that 'Some members of the political system seek to gain influence over the policies, rules, and decisions enforced by the government – i.e. political influence' (Dahl 1963, p. 16, italics in the original). The motivation to seek political influence is that 'control over the government' helps influential individuals 'achieve one or more of their own goals'.

Political influence is 'always distributed unevenly in political systems.' This is true because of the inequalities in distribution of resources already noted, but also because of 'variations in the *skill* with which different individuals use their political resources' and 'variations in the extent to which different individuals *use* their resources for political purposes'. (Dahl 1963, p. 17, italics in the original) And he notes that this process is circular because using your political resources skillfully can then lead to improvements in your political resources, motivations, and skills.

ROBERT A. DAHL

It is at this point that Dahl introduces the term 'leader'. He suggests that 'we call the individuals with the greatest political influence the *political leaders*'. And he notes that 'although the term "leader" has a great variety of meanings in ordinary language, whenever we speak of leaders or political leaders in this book we mean the individuals with the greatest influence in a political system'.

In the final step in this chain of reasoning, Dahl observes that 'leaders in a political system' try to ensure that most governmental decisions are accepted not just because of fear of punishment for non-compliance or the threat of coercion, but 'also from a belief that it is morally right and proper to do so'. What this boils down to is that 'leaders in a political system try to endow their actions with legitimacy'. When they succeed, their influence 'is usually referred to as *authority*'. And we can take it as a general rule that 'leaders in a political system try to convert their influence into authority' (Dahl 1963, p. 19, italics in the original).

Dahl reminds us that 'the individuals who find themselves within the boundaries of a political system are by no means equally concerned with political life'. Some citizens are indifferent, some are more deeply involved, but only a few of those 'actively seek power'. Even fewer actually gain it. He identifies four nested groups of citizens: 'the apolitical strata, the political strata, the power-seekers, and the powerful' (Dahl 1963, p. 56). He defines 'the political strata' as comprised of 'individuals who are psychologically "involved" in government decisions'. This involvement may be measured by degree of interest, concern, information, and activity, which are often correlated. In most political systems, the political strata 'are not a large proportion of the adults; generally, no doubt, they are a minority' even in a democratic society. In approaching democratic theory in this vein, Dahl departs markedly from the abstract egalitarian mood that characterized his writings before *Who Governs?* Not all citizens will be equally concerned with or involved in political life. In a working democracy, a minority of the citizens will be making the decisions that concern the common good.

In the final passages of this discussion, Dahl analyzes the motives and characteristics of the small minority of 'power seekers' and the even smaller minority who succeed in gaining it. He notes that there are many reasons why people might seek power, many different goals that may provide incentives to pursue it (Dahl 1963, p. 68). There are also, he says, many different personality characteristics that may be connected with this behavior. 'Undoubtedly both Caligula and Abraham Lincoln sought power. Yet it is highly implausible to suppose that Caligula and Lincoln had even approximately the same kind of personality' (Dahl 1963, p. 69).

Dahl closes the chapter by meditating on the difficult question why 'some people have more skill in politics than others'. There are 'three possible explanations': 'genetic differences, differences in opportunities to learn, and difference in incentives to learn'. The first two are 'differences in situations, the third is a difference in motivations' (Dahl 1963, p. 70).

Modern Political Analysis is Dahl's most systematic study of power, influence, and leadership. During the course of this brief but brilliant book, he touches on most of the factors that students of leadership across the centuries have identified as definitive in determining who will become a leader and who will succeed. Native talents, acquired skills, experience, and resources are all listed here. The factor conspicuous for its absence is what Machiavalli called *Fortuna*: the inscrutable good luck of being in the right place at the right time (Machiavelli 1988 [1532], pp. 84–87; chapter XXV). The reference to 'differences in situations' comes close, but the mood

ROBERT A. DAHL

of mysterious unpredictability about when fortune will favor a would-be leader is not part of Dahl's political universe.

Dahl's inattention to *Fortuna* reminds us of the importance of the political context within which theorists work. Machiavelli lived in a time of sudden changes in political regimes – the adverse effects of which he himself experienced. Dahl lived in a period of extraordinary stability as far as American politics was concerned. Throughout Dahl's working lifetime, the United States was a hegemonic power, exerting great impact on the world but relatively immune from adverse effects from outside our borders. In the period of his early work, until the mid-1960s, domestic politics was also uncommonly stable. Dahl paid little attention to *Fortuna* because *Fortuna* was smiling on his world.

Connections between leaders and other citizens

In his theoretical work in the early 1970s, Dahl regularly returned to the issue of leadership. The subtitle of *After the Revolution* is *Authority in a Good Society*, and in this deceptively informal but closely reasoned book, Dahl broaches several themes that are important to his theory of leadership.

The first half of this book explores 'three main criteria for judging whether I shall accept as valid and rightful, and therefore binding on me, a process for making decisions on matters that affect me' (Dahl 1970, p. 8). The first, most obvious reason for accepting a decision as rightful is that I have made the decision myself. This is the Criterion of Personal Choice. In his earliest work, Dahl had tried to identify a political system that will usually allow this criterion to prevail. But realistically, I will not make many of the political decisions made in any group of which I am a part and would not have chosen some of the outcomes. The challenge for a democratic political theorist is to show why I should accept the rightfulness of decisions that do not satisfy this criterion.

The second criterion, the Criterion of Competence, holds that if I believe that a person 'is particularly qualified by his knowledge or skill to render a correct judgment', I acknowledge this competence in accepting his authority (Dahl 1970, p. 28). A pilot and a physician are the examples; there is no direct reference to politics. But Dahl offers an especially important qualification here. Although we often say 'everyone should have the right to participate in decisions that affect his interests in a vital way', the fact that 'decisions on some matter affect your interests in a vital way does not mean that it is necessarily rational for you to insist on participating' (Dahl 1970, p. 31).

This argument is a softer version of the rejection of the Benthamite principle that 'I am always the best judge of my own interests', that we found in *Politics, Economics and Welfare*. Pursuing the theme in this context, Dahl takes up the issue of the competence of the 'ordinary man'. One's views on this topic, he says, are of the greatest importance for one's political philosophy. Democrats believe that an individual is usually 'more competent than anyone else to decide when and how much he shall intervene on decisions he feels are important to him' (Dahl 1970, p. 35, italics in the original). Despite the arguments that can be advanced in favor of expertise in government, Dahl remains in the democratic camp on this issue – but with markedly less confidence than he showed in his earlier work.

Dahl makes clear that to govern a state wisely, one needs not only competence, but also extraordinary virtue, to be able to set aside selfish interests, avoid the

ROBERT A. DAHL

seductive corrupting effects of power, and maintain the focus on the common good. He finds it implausible that any one individual (or group of individuals) could both exemplify this exceptional virtue and have sufficient expertise in the arts of governance to make better decisions for citizens than they can make for themselves. Dahl notes that 'the advocate of aristocracy in the realm of the state', as distinct from expertise in flying an airplane or conducting open-heart surgery,

> faces two formidable problems, for neither of which, so far as I know, is there a satisfactory solution. His minority of superior competence – the experts, wise men, guardians, or philosopher kinds – must somehow acquire and preserve both their *authority* and their *virtue*. (Dahl 1970, p. 36, italics in the original)

Despite his deep reservations, Dahl sees the arguments of his hypothetical aristocrat as sufficiently persuasive that 'the advocates of democracy', as well as the advocates of aristocracy, need to address 'some serious problems' with their positions. In their passionate commitment to popular sovereignty, democrats generally overstate the interest, competence, and involvement of most citizens. Aristocrats, in turn, have no way to assure us that 'a wise and virtuous aristocracy' will not become 'a cunning and voracious oligarchy'.

At this point, Dahl asserts that 'a single solution to both these problems might be to allow the citizens to elect a superior minority for a fixed term of office. This solution looks so much like a prescription for representative government', he continues, 'that doubtless it will frighten both the aristocrat and the democrat' (Dahl 1970, p. 37). Given someone as committed to participatory democracy as Dahl had been, it is striking that he finds this solution so persuasive. He does not pursue the argument at this point, but returns to it a few sections later.

The third criterion named by Dahl in *After the Revolution* is the Criterion of Economy (Dahl 1970, p. 76). Even if I am in principle committed to participating as fully as possible in the decisions that affect my interests, I will run up against limitations of both time and effort. I have only limited amounts of each of these resources, and there are many things I need and want to do in addition to participating in politics. Equally important, the mechanics of participation in a large group make it impossible for all members of a group to share equally in the decisions unless the group is very small. Thus, even the classical Greek assemblies and contemporary New England town meetings elect a chairman. They also appoint committees to set the agenda and other groups to implement decisions (Dahl 1970, pp. 42–45).

Recognizing the implications of the Criterion of Economy, Dahl uses arguments that quite a few theorists had advanced in earlier works. Rousseau, in the *Social Contract*, followed this same path to acknowledge the need for an executive. In this same mood, John Stuart Mill moved from a government that embodies popular sovereignty to representative government as the 'ideal type of a perfect government' (Mill 1962 [1861], p. 74). Following the same path to very different conclusions, Roberto Michels asserted the inevitability of oligarchy in *Political Parties*.

It is in this context that Dahl makes one of his most striking statements:

> When you begin to apply the Criterion of Economy to authority, you are soon driven to a discovery of very great importance: *What is an optimal system for making decisions is not necessarily what we ordinarily think of as* 'ideal'. *In fact, the optimal is almost always different from the ideal.* (Dahl 1970, p. 48, italics in the original)

With this admission, we come to another fork in the road for Dahl's discussion of democracy. His earliest theoretical works had confidently presented an ideal system, unconcerned by the fact that the criteria set forward were surely unobtainable in practice. At this point in his life, Dahl is more concerned with the optimal than the ideal.

In that mood, Dahl discusses four forms of democratic organization and authority: committee democracy, primary democracy, referendum democracy, and representative democracy. He notes that people throughout history have felt passionately about the superiority of one of these forms of government, but asserts that 'to hold that one of these forms of democracy is intrinsically better than another is nonsense' (Dahl 1970, p. 76). The goals, the conditions of the society, the levels of political interest and competence, the problems to be solved – all of these factors weigh in to determine which form is most suitable in particular circumstances. And the role of the 'professional politicians', the leaders and officers, increases as one moves up the scale of complexity and size.

In addition to these four forms of democratic organization, Dahl also describes a 'fifth form of authority ... that must be employed by all democratic states': various kinds of 'delegated authority'. He returns to the theme of leadership as 'delegation' that he and Lindblom broached in their co-authored book, and develops it a bit further. He notes that 'in a representative democracy the representatives are, in an abstract but important sense, delegated authorities', holding authority by delegation from the electors.

This idea could provide a fruitful basis for a theory of representative democracy, but Dahl pulls back once again from exploring the theme in depth. He is content to show how difficult it would be to instantiate a system of direct participation by all citizens in complex modern societies. He lets Rousseau in the *Social Contract* serve as the most effective advocate for primary democracy. Dahl notes that Rousseau's argument 'tends to distort reality by overlooking a vast body of concrete experience which shows that primary democracy, like polyarchy, is sure to witness the emergence of factions and leaders' (Dahl 1970, p. 82). In Dahl's reading, Rousseau tells us little about this topic except that 'these are evils to be avoided. Yet Rousseau should have known', Dahl goes on to say, 'that they are evils that cannot be avoided'.

Dahl is unfair to Rousseau, given the thoughtful discussions of the central work of the executive and government in the *Social Contract*, as well as the crucial role of the 'great-souled legislator'. But more important for our purposes, the fact that Dahl accepts this characterization of leadership in a democracy as a *necessary evil* is untrue to his own recognition of the place of leadership in a democratic polity. Dahl goes on to discuss Madison's solution for Rousseau's dilemma; recognizing that 'factions and leadership' will inevitably emerge, he saw that 'it was necessary to provide institutions for dealing with them' in a functioning republic. Given that leadership in a democracy 'cannot be avoided', the only solution is to contain it or 'deal with it' (Dahl 1970, p. 83).

This passage is an excellent indicator of why theorists of democracy have had so little to say about leadership. They have often shared this superficial understanding of 'leadership' as an 'evil' that must be confronted, or an anomaly that can safely be ignored, rather than a crucial part of the working of the system that must be handled wisely by those who design constitutions. Fortunately, Dahl usually avoided this pitfall.

ROBERT A. DAHL

Engaging in a thought-experiment about the 'Chinese boxes' that would be needed to construct a hypothetical global government and are essential to a working governmental system in a large nation state, Dahl observes that some of the boxes are less democratic than others. This is the only way, he says, that 'the people' can 'make their choices effective on matters of importance to them' (Dahl 1970, p. 93). Specifically, in a polyarchy, 'representative bodies must delegate authority still further to administrative bodies'. This step necessarily 'entails hierarchy'. He goes on to say:

> I do not see how we can stretch the meaning of 'democratic' authority to include the hierarchy of administration. Consequently we must conclude that rule by the people requires not only democratic forms but also non-democratic forms of delegated authority. (Dahl 1970, p. 94)

In concluding this passage, Dahl observes:

> Perhaps the greatest error in thinking about democratic authority is to believe that ideas about democracy and authority are simple and must lead to simple prescriptions. I hope you have seen why this cannot be so. If you do, than we could begin a dialog on how to develop democracy and rightful authority

at every level of our societies (Dahl 1970, p. 95).

Building on the concept of competence

In the final section of *After the Revolution*, Dahl moves 'from principles to problems'. Among other suggestions, he proposes that we might return to the ancient practice of selecting some representatives by lot. With the goal of 'democratizing the Leviathan', Dahl proposes creating 'advisory councils to every elected official of the giant polyarchy' we inhabit. Each council would 'consist of several hundred constituents' picked randomly by the procedures we use to ensure good sample surveys in social science (Dahl 1970, p. 149). The council would be chosen for one year, and meet at regular intervals for a total of several weeks. The official being advised would be expected to meet with the group, answer questions, and hear the debates.

The concept of bodies of ordinary citizens meeting to deliberate about specific issues has been advanced by other theorists of democracy including James Fishkin, and put into practice in several political jurisdictions around the world (Fishkin 2009). Advocates of these deliberative councils often give them decision-making power. This is a step that Dahl explicitly rejects. He says that the councils should be solely advisory because 'one hundred more or less average citizens snatched out of their daily lives by random selection would find the work of the United States Senate, for example, formidably complex'. However incompetent we may think our representatives are, through their experience in government, they acquire 'organizational know-how and substantive knowledge' that a random citizen could not possess (Dahl 1970, p. 151). This superior competence has nothing to do, Dahl says, with 'innate differences in abilities or capacities'. It arises from 'the very considerable amount of highly motivated learning that generally precedes and follows tenure in public office'. *This recognition of the competence acquired by ordinary citizens in positions of political authority is one important indication of why democratic theory needs to focus more specifically on leadership as a factor in democratic governance.*

Dahl takes another step in the same direction in *Polyarchy* (1971). In a fascinating postscript, he emphasizes the central role of political leadership in advancing the development of polyarchy. He imagines a 'hypothetical Innovator in a country governed by a hegemonic or mixed regime' who would like to move his country further along the way to 'full polyarchy' (Dahl 1971, p. 215). What steps should he take? The passages that follow include some of Dahl's most sustained discussions of what leadership means in a polity and how it might be used for the advantage of all citizens.

We cannot give our hypothetical Innovator any useful advice about 'how to acquire the power needed for political innovation in the context of a specific personal, national, and historical situation', or tactical issues such as reform or revolution, working with or against the existing regime, etc. Instead, Dahl focuses on 'questions of strategic objectives, of the specific ways in which power, once acquired, can be used in order to move closer to polyarchy in a particular country'.

The strategic advice is practical, focused, and thought-provoking. Among Dahl's precepts: fostering mutual tolerance among suspicious or hostile groups in the polity must be a paramount objective for the Innovator. Without this step, there is no hope of creating a polyarchal system in which power is shared and trust is essential. Dahl says that 'the costs of toleration can be lowered by effective mutual guarantees against destruction, extreme coercion, or severe damage' (Dahl 1971, p. 218).

Dahl notes also that in the use of executive authority, the Innovator must navigate a delicate transition from the old regime to the one he is attempting to establish. 'To reduce the likelihood of immobilism and deadlock, the executive must retain a considerable measure of power for rapid and decisive action, especially in emergencies'. For this purpose, the Innovator must have an 'authority that in a realistic sense is beyond the capacities of transitory majorities in parliament to curtail and yet not beyond the reach of influence of substantial and persistent coalitions, whether minorities or majorities' (Dahl 1971, p. 220).

The Innovator should search for 'a party system that avoids a great multiplication of parties'. This is because 'the costs of toleration are raised by excessive fragmentation into competing political parties' (Dahl 1971, p. 221). Dahl also recommends a layered system of government for this new polyarchy. Several different levels of government are more likely to facilitate this goal than a centralized regime. 'Somewhat autonomous representative institutions below the national level can provide opportunities for the opposition to acquire political resources, help to generate cross-cutting cleavages, and facilitate training in the arts of resolving conflicts and managing representative governments' (Dahl 1971, p. 226).

This guide to the Innovator is written in a mode reminiscent of Machiavelli's *Prince*: How should a new leader use power wisely to achieve his goals and sustain his authority? In the context of today's world, one cannot help but be struck by the many ways in which post-revolutionary heads of state have departed from the model Dahl provides. To name only a few of the most common difficulties: these new leaders have often counted on fragmentation to protect their own narrow political interests or those of their tribes. They have fostered mutual distrust instead of toleration. They have centralized rather than dispersed power. The heavy costs to their countries of civil conflict and unrest bear out the wisdom of Dahl's counsel.

ROBERT A. DAHL

Democracy and guardianship

In *Democracy and its Critics* (1989), Dahl confronts, at greater length, a bothersome issue that had woven through his earlier writings on democracy. How can we justify the sovereign exercise of political power by large groups of ordinary individuals, given the competence in governance gained by persons possessing unusual political resources, willing and able to use them skillfully? Dahl approaches this question by framing two hypothetical debates, showing how advocates of democracy must confront critics on two sides.

On the one hand, democrats must have good answers to those who argue for anarchy, those who believe that 'coercion is intrinsically bad', and thus that all states are 'inherently evil' (Dahl 1989, p. 37). Anarchists assert that the best system is one in which individuals pursue a spontaneous coordination of their goals and interests, rather than being forced to obey external authority and submit to coercion. Dahl gives Anarchos only a brief chapter in which to make his case, quickly demolished. This section stands as a thought-provoking refutation of the arguments of contemporary democratic theorists, who believe that the most desirable instantiation of democracy is one that moves as close as possible to anarchy – i.e. no state, no coercion, no leadership.

It proves considerably more difficult to dispose of the advocate of Guardianship, Aristos, who has a strongly Platonic heritage. He denies that 'ordinary people can be counted on to understand and defend their own interests – much less the interests of the larger society'. Instead, 'rulership should be entrusted to a minority of persons who are specially qualified to govern by reason of their superior knowledge and virtue' (Dahl 1989, p. 52). The argument turns on the understanding of 'competence' and 'expertise' and how these factors are distributed in human societies. This involves both 'competence' as the ability to make good decisions and also the possession of enough 'moral competence' to be willing and able to look beyond your own narrow interests to consider the needs of others, and think about what is good for the entire society.

Demos – the advocate for democracy – contends that 'an adequate level of moral competence is widely distributed among human beings, and in any case no distinctively superior moral elite can be identified or safely entrusted with power to rule over the rest' (Dahl 1989, p. 59). Aristos has no trouble providing multiple examples of how people generally 'lack much understanding of their own basic needs, interests or good'. He also asserts that 'most people find it difficult, perhaps impossible, to take the good of others – very many others, anyway – into account in making decisions' (Dahl 1989, p. 60). His guardians would 'be experts in the art of governing', given that 'ruling is only one specialized activity among a great many'. This argument from the division of labor dates back to the *Republic* and the *Statesman* dialogs, where Plato treats ruling as a distinctive expertise, more like piloting a ship than engaging in casual social activities. 'In a well-ordered society', says Aristos, some persons 'would be rigorously trained and selected to function well as rulers' (Dahl 1989, p. 63).

Asked by Demos to come up with examples of polities where this has actually worked, Aristos names the Republic of Venice, Florence under the Medici, and Confucian China during periods of stability and prosperity. Demos replies rather lamely that he doesn't see that such 'historical examples are relevant to today's world', but admits that Aristos has sketched out 'a powerful vision. It has always been the strongest competitor to the democratic vision and remains so today' (Dahl 1989, p. 64).

In the following chapter, Dahl speaks in his own voice to make his best case for democracy. He asserts that 'both moral understanding and instrumental knowledge are always necessary for policy judgments', and 'it is precisely here that any argument for rule by a purely technocratic elite must fail'. Good *judgment*, informed by moral precepts, is basic to good governance. There is no reason to suppose that highly trained technocrats can make such judgments any better than anyone else – and perhaps less well (Dahl 1989, p. 69). Note that in this section, Dahl has shifted the ground of the argument from a set of leaders *trained in the expertise of governing*, which would presumably include honing the faculty of judgment, to technocratic experts, which is quite a different set.

The argument continues with an exploration of whether individuals are best qualified to make judgments about matters that concern their own interests. Dahl goes over familiar ground in this discussion. But the introduction of the concept of *judgment*, which many scholars of leadership would regard as the most distinctive component of political leadership, is a new and promising theme (Keohane 2010, pp. 87–94, 181–84) Dahl's discussion of judgment is quite brief, but for anyone who has pondered the conundrums of democratic leadership, it is a suggestive thread to follow.

Conclusion

Dahl never developed a sustained theory of leadership. Nonetheless, his writings include a number of ideas that could be incorporated into a richer theory. He poses the question of how we think about leadership in a democracy at the most basic level: Are leaders controlling (or controlled?) If so, what methods do they use to exercise control, and over whom? And how, and by whom, are they controlled? Instead of referring to *control*, is it more helpful to say that leaders in a democracy bring exceptional *influence* to bear in making decisions? And if so, whom or what are they influencing?

Both the concepts of *control* and *influence* miss some prominent facets of what it means to provide leadership in a democracy. There are also references in Dahl's work to the most distinctive aspect of leadership: taking *initiative*. When we consider politics in terms of leadership, we usually think about initiatives and agenda-setting, which goes well beyond what Dahl and Lindblom called 'endorsing, facilitating or vetoing' ideas. Agenda-setting, bargaining, and taking initiative were among the themes that Dahl broached in *Who Governs?* That venture into exploring 'retail politics' had a very beneficent effect on his understanding of democratic governance.

Dahl's work includes a sure sense of the importance of access to political resources and their skillful use for effective action in any political system. If we link this insight more closely to leadership than he did, we can explore more fully what counts as an effective 'political resource' for leaders in particular situations and how and why individuals differ in their motivations to exercise leadership and in the skill with which they use resources to guide and energize others.

The identification of leadership in a democracy with a pattern of unequal resources, in which some citizens have more resources than others and therefore have the 'greatest influence' on decisions, has significant consequences for political equality. Theorists of democracy since Aristotle (as well as critics since Plato) have emphasized the importance of equality among citizens in a democracy. If some citizens have and use more resources than others, and thereby come to have greater influence – an observation surely borne out in any democracy we know – then what happens to equality?

The most striking evolution in Dahl's concept of leadership is from the *Preface to Democratic Theory* – in which citizens are identical faceless units with equal access to agenda-setting and influence over decisions – to *Modern Political Analysis* – in which disparities in political resources and thus political influence are always unequally distributed in a democracy. *Who Governs?* – the key intervening work between these two analytical treatises – demonstrates how leaders and citizens can reciprocally influence one another, and makes clear how auxiliaries or subleaders are essential in the democratic process.

In *After the Revolution,* Dahl shows how the Criterion of Economy produces a division of labor in any society. Non-stop engagement in politics is both unappealing to many citizens and technically impossible. One facet of this specialization will be the greater involvement of some citizens in politics compared to others. Given this greater involvement, those citizens will use resources to bring to bear greater influence, to have more control over decisions in the polity. For all these reasons, perfect political equality is inevitably an illusion, as Dahl shows. Because leadership in a democracy is associated with a pattern of unequal resources, there are always tensions between leadership and political equality.

Yet perhaps this inevitable inequality is not entirely a drawback. Does it make sense, after all, for each of us always to want to have the final say over the significant decisions in our lives? The Criterion of Competence reminds us that there are many types of issues where it is wiser to delegate those decisions to someone else, someone who knows more about the subject than we do. Thus, unlike many theorists, Dahl is willing to entertain the possibility that expertise in governance has relevance in a democracy. He came to this conclusion late in his work, and somewhat reluctantly; but he recognized that the possession of political resources, experience in exercising power, and acquired skill in making decisions mean that some citizens are better prepared than others to provide leadership in a healthy democracy.

However, Dahl remained firm in his belief that this insight does not entail the conclusion that those who are prepared to lead and willing to devote time and energy to doing so are 'better' than the rest of us. Nor should we simply turn over all aspects of governing to these leaders. They are surely not immune from the ordinary failings we all share as human beings and from others that especially infect those who wield power. These 'expert leaders' may very probably become 'cruel and vicious autocrats' unless strong limits are set on their exercise of authority. Dahl was committed, throughout his life, to the essential principles of popular sovereignty and abstract political equality. And he remained convinced that such principles can be instantiated in the form of government he called 'polyarchy'.

The final theme Dahl broaches in his late work is the importance of good *judgment* in effective governance. He asserts that 'both moral understanding and instrumental knowledge are always necessary for policy judgments'. Unfortunately, he did not develop this idea further, but he reminds us that this elusive faculty of judgment is one of the factors that must be explored in any satisfactory theory of political leadership. Good judgment – canny, perceptive, experienced, intuitive, informed by moral precepts – is basic to good governance.

All these insights – control or influence, the possession and use of resources, the reciprocal relationships between leaders and citizens, taking initiative, developing competence, demonstrating expertise and good judgment – help us understand some crucial facets of leadership in a democracy. Yet Dahl was always firm in his belief that such leadership must not be allowed to undermine the fundamental principle of popular sovereignty. *Democracy and its Critics*, after chronicling in great detail the multiple impediments and difficulties that attend any attempt to bring popular sovereignty into practical reality in a working polyarchy, concludes with this ringing statement:

> Yet the vision of people governing themselves as political equals, and possessing all the resources and institutions necessary to do so, will I believe remain a compelling if always demanding guide in the search for a society in which people may live together in peace, respect each other's intrinsic equality, and jointly seek the best possible life. (Dahl 1989, p. 341)

Accepting the power of this vision while also understanding that this goal cannot be accomplished without sound political leadership – both in founding and in sustaining such a polity – is the challenge that now faces us as we attempt to construct a more comprehensive theory of leadership in a democracy.

Disclosure statement

No potential conflict of interest was reported by the author.

References

Arendt, H., 1958. *The human condition*. Chicago, IL: University of Chicago Press.
Aristotle, 1962. *In*: E. Barker, ed. *Politics*. New York: Oxford University Press.
Baldwin, D., 1979. Power analysis and world politics: new trends versus old tendencies. *World Politics*, 31 (2) January, 161–194.
Dahl, R.A., 1956. *A preface to democratic theory*. Chicago, IL: University of Chicago Press.
Dahl, R.A., 1957. The concept of power. *Behavioral Science*, 2 (3) July, 201–215.
Dahl, R.A., 1961. *Who governs? Democracy and power in an American city*. New Haven, CT: Yale University Press.
Dahl, R.A., 1963. *Modern political analysis*. Englewood Cliffs, NJ: Prentice-Hall.
Dahl, R.A., 1970. *After the revolution: authority in a good society*. New Haven, CT: Yale University Press.

ROBERT A. DAHL

Dahl, R.A., 1971. *Polyarchy: participation and opposition*. New Haven, CT: Yale University Press.

Dahl, R.A., 1982. *Dilemmas of pluralist democracy: autonomy vs. control*. New Haven, CT: Yale University Press.

Dahl, R.A., 1989. *Democracy and its critics*. New Haven, CT: Yale University Press.

Dahl, R.A. and Lindblom, C.E., 1953. *Politics, economics and welfare: planning and politico-economic systems resolved into basic social processes*. New York: Harper & Row.

Fishkin, J., 2009. *When the people speak: deliberative democracy and public consultation*. Oxford: Oxford University Press.

Gardner, J.W., 1990. *On leadership*. New York: Free Press.

Ignatieff, M., 2013. *Fire and ashes*. Toronto: Random House Canada.

Keohane, N.O., 2010. *Thinking about leadership*. Princeton, NJ: Princeton University Press.

Machiavelli, N., 1988 [1532]. *In*: Q. Skinner and R. Price, eds. *The prince*. Cambridge: Cambridge University Press.

Mill, J.S., 1962 [1861]. *Considerations on representative government*. Chicago, IL: Henry Regnery.

Rousseau, J.-J., 1997 [1762]. *In*: V. Gourevitch, ed. *The social contract and other later political writings*. Cambridge: Cambridge University Press.

Dahl's feminism?

Catharine A. MacKinnon[a,b]

[a]*Elizabeth A. Long Professor of Law, University of Michigan, Ann Arbor, MI, USA;* [b]*The James Barr Ames Visiting Professor of Law (long-term), Harvard Law School, Cambridge, MA, USA*

> This tribute to the life work of Robert A. Dahl briefly analyzes the place of women, and issues raised by the status and treatment of women, in the sweep of his iconic contributions to democratic theory. The article traces his inclusion of women from the beginning to the end of his writings on politics in democracies and, in a more critical vein, casts light on some central concepts in his work that the insights and information of feminist scholarship would deepen, modify, or question.

Robert Dahl was democratic not only in theory but in practice. Sponsor of offbeat student projects, he practiced pluralism. Humble and candid, he was transparent and accountable, temperate but pointed, his mellow lucidity and sharp logic models of rationality in a common voice, talking with you like an equal, like a friend.

Bob Dahl single-handedly saved me from being kicked out of graduate school, hired me as his TA, first put me in front of a classroom full of students and told me afterwards that I could teach, referred me to his own publisher for what became my first book, advised my dissertation, did not see or treat me as a traitor for going to law school, and was always there for the next 25 years – making that a total of 40 years.

Sailing down off the ridge on his bicycle for our meetings in his office, he made sure I did not overlook the role of luck and chance for any simple determinism. Against my assertion that there were no accidents or coincidences in political life, he said that, with bombs falling and shells flying, nothing determined the fact that this one fell here, that one fell over there, so he was alive and the rest of his company was killed in the war. In print, he later theorized emerging from battle with your life as 'sheer luck', (Dahl 1996, p. 639), a factor he connected with the life chances of human beings that depend upon contingencies of birth (p. 640).

Bounding radiant off the tennis court one day in his whites, maybe in summer 1974, presented with three options for my thesis – the third, a full-dress political theory for the women's movement from epistemology to law and the state, from knowledge to power – he took a beat and said, 'I think you should do the one on women'. So I did.[1] His rapier theoretical mind, astute point-blank assessments, and gentle penetrating questions were always directed toward making the work better on its own terms. All this had always seemed remarkable, even miraculous. But although I had of course read his work, I didn't think to look there for what had made such a difference in my life until after Bob died.

His autobiography on growing up in Skagway, Alaska, takes a measure of feminism from his mother: 'In her own way, she was, I think, something of a feminist. I don't think she ever doubted that women were as intelligent, resourceful, and competent as men' (Dahl 2005a, p. 11). I don't think he ever doubted it either. The most striking fact that emerges from reading Bob Dahl's oeuvre for its feminism is that virtually nothing he wrote from 1951 to 2006 fails to notice women, including our absence, in politics. Women's absence was noticed rather than overlooked; the forms that presence could take were sometimes quantified and analyzed as integral to the political process. His generic 'man' of 1947 (Dahl 1947, p. 7), perhaps understandable in a piece on public administration, never really reappears. From then on, women or women's exclusion were, with a taken-for-granted tone, effortlessly part of this man's democracy, from the 'he or she' of his political actors to the repeated quiet factual characterization of the American legal and political status quo as 'white male'.[2]

A typical if especially nice example of his open gender neutrality, given that the subject is widely (if questionably) considered lacking gender dimension, occurs in his discussion of nuclear weapons (Dahl 1985, p. 59). When he criticizes Rousseau for obscurity and illogic, he notes: 'The collective grows larger, the individual shrinks – in influence, power, liberty, capacity for shaping the laws to which he or she is subject' (Dahl 1970, p. 76), even if this obscures whether collectivity has the same effect on shrinking women's individual political potency as it does men's. If a good many generic 'human beings' populate his work, so too do 'men and women', for example, 'The theoretical vision of democracy focuses on men as citizens – more lately, men and women as citizens' (Dahl 1986, p. 8).

Exploring public control, he noticed the participation of women's groups in his 1951 monograph (Dahl and Brown 1951, p. 9). His classic 1961 *Who Governs?*, the study of political power in New Haven, repeatedly observes the contributions of women's organizations as well as of women as voters (Dahl 1961, pp. 266, 313, 338), as does his *Pluralist Democracy in the United States: Conflict and Consent* (Dahl 1967, p. 133). The subsequent explosive growth and 'changes in attitudes and concerns' in women's mobilization as citizen interest groups in the years that followed left some tracks in his later work (Dahl 1994, p. 8). But even in his early analysis of leadership, one encounters this:

> In a society where public life is still widely thought to be a man's world and where men rather than women are generally expected to occupy the positions of responsibility, it is not surprising that two-thirds of the subleaders are men. But they are distinguished by more than merely the conventional privileges of American manhood. (Dahl 1961, p. 177)

Men are observed *as men* almost a decade before *Sexual Politics* (Millett 1969) ('sex has a frequently neglected political aspect'), their gender analyzed as part of the operation of the political system. Who said this kind of thing then?

Women's status was most frequently explicitly discussed together with that of slaves as examples of disenfranchisement, noninclusiveness of citizenship, deprivation of personal autonomy, assumptions of incompetence, denial of legal rights, and failure of representation – all central themes of his work as a democratic theorist.

ROBERT A. DAHL

He observed that women had legally long been 'essentially the property of their fathers and husbands' (Dahl 2006a, p. 19). In interrogating who are 'the people' of a democracy, 'or rather *a* people – and hence are entitled to govern themselves in their *own* association' (Dahl 1970, p. 46) – a topic he saw had been largely neglected in classical political theory[3] – Dahl criticized (*inter alia*) Rousseau, in his discussion of procedural democracy, for 'assum[ing] that a large number of persons [including] women will be subjects but are not qualified to be citizens' (1986, p. 209).[4] Locke, he contended, despite a categorical and universalistic language of civic inclusiveness, almost certainly did not mean to include women as participants, but rather regarded them as subject to 'paternal power' (Dahl 1986, p. 209 and n. 10, p. 279). The notion that adult women were not competent to pursue their own fundamental interests '*but also that a class of paternalistic authorities could be counted on to do so in their behalf*', italics his, was pointedly criticized as 'comprehensive paternalism' (Dahl 1985, pp. 58–59).

Tocqueville, Bob never failed to say when speaking of his work (which was frequently), neglected women as citizens and voters, making his 'a democracy among American white males' (Dahl 1956, p. 11), an indictment that became stronger and legally focused by the time of his 1988 Tanner Lectures: 'the republic founded by the Constitution was at most a white male republic' (Dahl 1989b, p. 57). This analysis, visible in *After the Revolution?* (1970), grew to become a focus of his 'shadow theory of democracy' in *Democracy and Its Critics* (Dahl 1989a). There, he fully took on the tacit antidemocratic assumption lurking behind democratic theory from its Greek origins through its most celebrated later advocates that government by the people really only meant some people. Specifically, it meant 'that only some people are competent to rule' (Dahl 1989a, p. 4), women presumptively excluded as not competent, and thus effectively not people within the theorized meaning. Further illustrations of this simple but marked nonforgetting can be found in Bob's book, *Polyarchy*, which otherwise discusses women virtually not at all, where he notes that few would argue that Switzerland is democratic 'yet the feminine half of the Swiss population is still excluded from national elections' (1971, p. 5), and in *On Political Equality*, when he observed that in 1900, of the eight countries that were then basically representative democracies, only in New Zealand could women vote (2006a, p. 23). Simply having women register, women's existence not be wholly overlooked, is at once ridiculously trivial and incalculably monumental.

Dahl went further than bracketing the demographic when he asked, 'does anyone really believe today that when the working classes, women, and racial and ethnic minorities were excluded from political participation their interests were adequately considered and protected by those who were privileged to govern them?' (2006a, p. 5). This question about adequacy of representation goes also to legitimacy. In 1985, he asked more pointedly of the consequences of this privilege of paternalism, 'Do we have the slightest reason for believing that slaves and women would not have protected their own interests at least as well as their masters – and in all likelihood far better?' (Dahl 1985, pp. 59–60). So, did the masters who owned slaves and women rule to protect their own interests over them? And might these excluded groups have brought something to governing beyond their own self-interests? By 2005, Bob had extended his critique of Toqueville to a broader indictment: '[I]n countries that were otherwise more or less democratic, as in America, a full half of all adults were completely excluded from national political life simply because they were women', as integral to his conclusion that 'our existing political institutions display many shortcomings' and need to advance the demos and the polis beyond polyarchy (Dahl 2005b, p. 191). In the theoretical life project of Robert Dahl, women were no exception, footnote, or afterthought. Marginally included, is how I would describe it.

Although sex is uncritically treated as a 'difference' throughout his analysis of equality, as race for example is not, he treated whatever 'differences' of sex may matter for politics as social, not biological, and saw they are socially exaggerated. One early instance of this is:

> The fact that men are, on the average, physically larger and stronger than women means that men have access to more direct, primitive, physical force. And it may well be that the historic subordination of women to men is determined in large part by the fact that in a knock-down fight, men would ordinarily emerge victorious. Many endowments such as wealth, social standing, or the level of education and aspiration of one's parents, are not biological, however, but social. Whatever their source, differences in biological and social endowments at birth often multiply into even greater differences in resources among adults. (Dahl 1963, p. 15)

Although Dahl never gave any political weight or legitimacy to this differentiation – one that was and is rather widely assumed to be valid – its lack of logic and ideological function as rationalization for subordination is evident from the obvious observation that bigger and stronger men do not systematically have more political or social power than smaller and weaker men do. His treatment of sex as a difference can be a bit imploded. For example, 'There are good warriors and poor warriors; some men are eloquent, some are not. There are men – and women' (Dahl and Lindblom 1953, p. 280). And so? If this passage with Lindblom could be read to suggest that, in his view, women are to men as poor warriors and speakers are to good ones, his 1996 essay 'Equality versus Inequality' definitively offers a political analysis to the contrary. As inequalities that cumulate into stable systems, slavery and the subordination of women are described as:

> systems of dominance and severe inequality that were institutionalized and enforced by an overwhelming array of the most powerful forces available. These include individual and collective terror and violence, official and unofficial; law, custom, and convention; social and economic structures. (Dahl 1996, p. 643)

Adding religion, he concluded: 'these formidable forces were backed up by the state itself' (p. 643). The only quibble here might be with the past tense.

As a sidelight, many of Bob's telescoped insights fused with unabashed normativity on other topics might felicitously be repurposed to illuminate the political situation of women in ways he never imagined. His 1955 observation of the uselessness of the theory/science debate on 'what is political science' – a discussion in which 'bones of old skeletons are rattled with such furious energy that one has the momentary illusion of life' (Dahl 1955, p. 479) – puts one in mind of the tedious and ideological nature/nurture debate on what accounts for sex inequality. His later reflections on why he wrote the *Preface* (1956) vividly evokes much legal argument, including on sex: 'Trying to come to grips with [it] … was often like digging for soft-shell clams: the harder I dug the more the argument seemed to disappear into the sand' (Dahl 1991, p. 297). His doctoral dissertation pungently characterizing restraints on capitalism, such as laws restricting women's night work, as 'the new liberalism hop[ing] to dam a river with a fence' (Dahl 1940, p. 111) brings to mind nothing so much as the law of rape.

How does his work stand up by feminist standards? Revisiting his treatment of questions central both to his work and to feminist scholarship reveals that issues for democratic theory raised by sex and gender inequality did not capture Robert Dahl's extended attention. When he spoke of the life chances of human beings that depend upon contingencies of birth (Dahl 1996, p. 640), sex was not among them, although if anything is 'sheer luck', the sex one is assigned at birth is with profound life-long consequences. If he did not assert that the extension of suffrage solved everything, his observation that 'the inclusive principles of the Declaration proved more enduring than the exclusionary practices, and the fundamental political right of "all men" – meaning all adult persons – to be included in the demos has been successfully, if belatedly, established' (Dahl 1980, p. 565) is overly sanguine so far as women are concerned. He never examined the difference the extension of the franchise to women did and did not make, despite its status as a natural experiment in democracy. One place for this might have been *How Democratic is the American Constitution?*, in which he notes that initially 'a woman's vote [counted] for nothing, zero' (Dahl 2001, p. 47) and later that 'women were enfranchised' (p. 128). The discussion of the relation between rights and outcomes for the people granted those rights is discussed in some detail for African-Americans there (p. 128), but not for women. Of expansions of political rights, he wrote that, 'Thanks to these expansions of political equality, women and Blacks are today rightly influential in American political life' (Dahl 2006b, p. 468), yet correctly qualified this observation by noting the persistence of relative inequality of these same groups. It is curious that a tension this clear and crucial is not explored in systematic depth or detail. What if the 'white male' character of the political system is far deeper than a demographic description of its original shapers and predominant occupants and reaches its rules, norms, and structures?

Analysis of power was central to Bob's work. His treatment in the *Preface* begins, in substance, with discussion of a hypothesis of Madisonian democracy: 'If unrestrained by external checks, any given individual or group of individual will tyrannize over others' (Dahl 1956, p. 6).[5] As to how we know this, and whether it is accurate or a correct initial premise for democratic government, his discussion does not include questioning whether this has been true of men's power over women or whether women have ever exercised such unchecked power over men – in other words, whether the hypothesis conceals gendered assumptions about reality beneath its gender neutral universality. If it is accurate for some men's rule over all women and other men, democratic theory harbors a presumed but fundamental gendered dimension. One would think it matters, a massive shadow in democracy's theory. The uncomfortable fact remains that men's power over women – in the context of rape and battering, it is no exaggeration to term tyranny – remains demonstrably largely unchecked, including in democracies. Exposed for its gendered content, this concealed dimension potentially lurks in Dahl's subsequent identification of a First Condition for constitutionally prescribed authority to be nontyrannical: 'The accumulation of all powers ... in the same hands, whether of one, a few, or many ... must be avoided'. Neither the Federalist, from which he draws this, nor Dahl (1956, p. 11, quoting Federalist No. 47 1788) discloses even a glimmer of imagining that the sameness of these proto-tyrannical hands could include their sex.

ROBERT A. DAHL

Bob's alternative and preferred conceptualization of power describes 'a more realistic relationship, such as A's capacity for acting in such a manner as to control B's responses' (Dahl 1956, p. 13). His later definition in *Democracy and Its Critics* distinguishes power from authority as 'the ability to compel compliance through the use or threat of force' (Dahl 1989a, p. 42), thus centering the definition more directly on coercion and looking to the concept on domination. Suppose A, by means of sexually abusing B in childhood, makes B into someone who does what A, and people like A, wants without the need of further physical force. Is this an exercise of power? Is it domination? If so, masculinity is a form of tyranny, as yet generating no library of political theory as a restraint on democracy. Realizing that conservatively counted 38% of girls report being sexually abused before they reach the age of majority (Russell 1983), and among its consequences can be experiencing validation and approval when being violated, the political questions raised for the nature of power – as it cumulates into the social hierarchies of masculinity over femininity, hence men over women that are then replicated structurally across the more conventionally recognized political system – make Bob's definition of power look relatively superficial and atomistic. His analysis of how societies of modern dynamic pluralism inhibit the concentration of power, and how such a dispersal of power prevents unilateral domination and coercion (see, e.g. Dahl 1989a, pp. 252–253) proceeds unaware of such rather massive contraindications. We are talking about over half the population here.

Lukes's notion of ideological power comes closer to the feminist mark in observing the role of dominant social groups in shaping norms and values held by others (see Lukes 1974, esp. pp. 26–28), despite theorizing a narrower sense of the political and the power that infuses and drives it than the women's movement (see MacKinnon 1989) produced. Seeing gender as a conflict is also missed. While taking Bob to task, it should be mentioned that nobody has yet actually theorized the issues of gender inequality, and, in particular, issues of sexual abuse, raise for power as such in democratic theory or otherwise. Some have centered their attention on a version of the question but elided its reality almost entirely hence gotten nowhere. For instance, the more Butler (1997) talks about power, the more gender, far less inequality, recedes from view, despite the mention of child abuse (pp. 7–8). Others have raised the question of gender as a form of power in promising settings but ultimately sidelined and buried its reality and implications (see, e.g. Allen 2010). Yet, others have theorized a dimension of power that encompasses domination through the creation of social subjects for which gender could have been a – even the – central illuminating instance, but was not, one result being airbrushing force and fear (see, e.g. Haugaard 2012). Sexual abuse in any real sense is all but indiscernible in this literature.

In a connected vein, Dahl's fairly uncritical if more extensive treatment of consent in democratic theory is also uncontextualized by social realities such as sex. Bob offered that hunter-gatherers, by depending on consent (more like a kind of consensus), were democratic, making democracy the oldest form of government (Dahl 1989a, p. 232), neglecting to notice that societies of hunter-gatherers were thought in research at the time to be relatively sex-equal, although both their general and sex-based egalitarianism have come under serious challenge since, without calling for his re-evaluation.[6] Taking *Democracy and Its Critics* (Dahl 1989a) as exemplary, he discussed how consent to be governed could be expressed through representatives (p. 28), arguing that regarding anarchism that 'true consent would have to be continuous' (p. 50); considered that rule by guardianship embodies the belief that 'at its best a system might actually rest on the consent of all' (p. 64, for Aristo); considered that for Rousseau and Locke, consent balanced the attractiveness of self-governance with the necessity of living in association with others (p. 89); and explored how states can enforce laws on noncitizens, who have given no explicit or implicit consent to be governed (p. 120). As elsewhere, he examined Locke and Rousseau's slide from their initial belief that formation of government required unanimous consent of everyone subjected to it to their devolution into majority rule, implicitly predicating their justifications on contingent judgments of the relative qualifications of a person to participate (pp. 122–126). He examined the vicissitudes of political autonomy as an absolute right within the framework of consent to be governed (pp. 196–197) and asserted it was critical for establishment of the US Government (p. 274).

Unmentioned was that no known woman consented to the establishment of the US Government or had the opportunity to meaningfully dissent from it. One is left wondering whether his analysis of how political formulas used by ruling classes to justify their domination usually results in rules that govern with the consent of the governed (Dahl 1989a, p. 275) apply to whether women meaningfully consent either to existing governments in which they had no formative and little on-going voice or to the rule of men as a social sex class. Meantime, consent is operationalized in courts adjudicating rape as if democracy is not being enacted or limited there on a daily basis, discussion of which is confined to the legal literature through a vacuum boundary between law and politics, even as both tend to relegate the topic to the gender ghetto.

His study of the role of apathetic majorities in the intensity question similarly missed the significance of the fact that women are the majority of adults, with perhaps distinctive reasons for apathy, although he noticed 'markedly less voting (for a variety of reasons)' among women, to whom the franchise was recently expanded, than among men (Dahl 1967, p. 69). In the *Preface*, he concluded that the Supreme Court cannot solve certain problems due to its inability to resolve the intensity issue, specifically that judicial review does not prevent the preferences of relatively intense minorities from being overridden by apathetic majorities without also, undemocratically, restraining intense majorities (1956, pp. 111–112). With regard to regulation of women's wages and hours, he notes that 'the Supreme Court effectively delayed an apparently intense law-making majority for as much as a quarter of a century' (p. 111). If women are this apparently intense law-making majority, this analysis lacks depth and specificity. At the time, women had little real voice in any sector that debated whether or how their wages and hours would be regulated. The Supreme Court did not tend to see itself as a representative body. The working class, including working women, was deeply divided on the proper approach to this problem. Many thought that solving it for women only would keep them a second-class sector of the labor force. The Supreme Court *allowed* regulation of women's wages and hours but not men's, a decision many found demeaning and others found a material relief (Compare *Muller v. Oregon*, 208 US 412 (1908) with *Lochner v. New York*, 198 US 45 (1905)). Thus, delayed were legislative and judicial prohibitions on sex discrimination – by half a century. Similarly, speaking of a lack of sense of efficacy and alienation from political power, Bob observed sex-based variance (see, e.g. Dahl and Tufte 1973, pp. 49, 62), but did not explore any of its gendered dimensions, whether historical and structural or products of on-going culture, socialization, and discrimination. The particulars matter.

More generally, women being a majority of adults, yet both socially and politically unequal to men and documented to have some distinctive voting and nonvoting patterns, their example might have been particularly fruitful for interrogating the theory of majority rule. An article titled 'Reflections on Human Nature and Politics: From Genes to Political Institutions' might have pondered questions of sex and gender, along with Hitler and Mao (Dahl 2006c), as offering a comparative perspective on its central concepts. Bob might also have explored the significance of the facts that slaves and women overlap empirically as well as conceptually, so are not really two separate groups, and that the family as a unit is small in size while being very far from democratic. That his notion of the family was a bit rosily ideological rather than politically informed or data-based, while not failing to notice it is small, is suggested by his reference to the family as an exemplary site of altruism: '[M]ost altruism occurs in small, usually very small, groups. The prototypical example is the family' (Dahl 1996, p. 642). If only.

Bob was consistently critical of the US Constitution, including comparing it unfavorably with those of other mature democracies by the measure of women's representation in Cabinets and among the unemployed (Dahl 2002). The absence of an explicit guarantee of women's rights in the US Constitution might, in parallel comparative vein, have productively been contrasted with its presence in various forms in over 186 world constitutions (see MacKinnon 2012). What, he might have asked, does this mean, portend, and prevent? Instead, he apparently thought that the absence of an Equal Rights Amendment in the US Constitution was compensated for by expansion in interpretation of the Fourteenth Amendment (Dahl 2001, p. 28), which is not the case.[7] This, despite quoting with approval Rogers Smith saying that the US Constitution 'left intact institutions that denied women legal and political privileges' (Dahl 2006a, p. 19). Bob repeatedly urged structural change in the US political system, including a wider public discussion of 'alternative arrangements that could make our political system fairer and more democratic' (Dahl 2002), without once discussing gender parity as one such possible structural change – an approach using reservations or quotas variously being taken (by 2014 on my count) in 113 countries and productively examined by many women political scientists.[8] Given exclusion from the design of purportedly democratic institutions, and continued marginalization within them, will women ever be equal to men in democracies without such a structural change, tabooed in US political discourse? Wasn't this question right up his alley?

His magisterial *Politics, Economics, and Welfare* (1953) with Lindblom noticed, but did not really analyze or explore, the politics of the economic inequality of the sexes, specifically the impact of distinctively sex-based poverty on women's political voice, participation, and power. Granted, this was Mad Men 1953, but the consequences of women's economic inequality not only for democracy in principle but for its structure and policy outputs in practice might have stimulated some fine-grained empirically informed analysis as time went on. This is integral to his lack of focus, at any length or in any depth, on the continuing structural consequences of centuries of women's marginalization in the demos as well as exclusion from the polis, either for its effects on them or on the political system itself. The level of abstraction of his work does not contend with such concrete matters, despite his intense interest in every conceptual dimension they illustrate. For example, although Bob marks in passing the issue of campaign finance as intractable (Dahl 2006b, p. 469), he does not connect it with the persistent structural economic inequality of the sexes and the failure of the legal and constitutional system in American democracy to remedy that inequality, resulting in sex-based political inequality in practice.

While women's poverty has long been an obvious political problem in electoral systems that run on money, since 2010, the *Citizens United* ruling has prohibited government under the First Amendment from restricting independent political expenditures by nonprofit corporations (*Citizens United v. Federal Election Commission*, 558 US 310 (2010)), a ruling extended to for profit and other associations, making the situation markedly worse. As a matter of political economy, this ruling has further empowered American economic elites as never before, elites who are largely men, men who have showed disinclination to fund women candidates on a par with men. Sex differential lack of command of financial resources might thus be observed to be an increasingly serious problem for the representativeness of democracy, both for poor people in general and for specific groups like women who are impoverished as such. Surely a theory that focuses the links between economics and politics is interested in this. If economics ever counted for politics, surely it counts here, with essentially half of the demos systematically impoverished in resources based on sex alone, even as money comes to count for more and more in elections, with less and less accountability or transparency in their financial manipulation. Bob's exploration of the effect of the distribution of resources on the ability to influence and participate in the democratic process[9] remains, with much else on a high level of abstraction, ignoring such a concrete elephant in the room, granted that the capstone case itself came very late in his life. But is Dahl's observation that 'In practice, market capitalism makes political equality all but impossible to achieve' (Dahl 1996, p. 646), all that can be said or done on this? Might countering its sex-based discrimination offer a way in?

Finally, in asking whether international organizations can be democratic (Dahl 1999), Bob neglected to see that women are arguably better and more responsively represented in and by them than in or by any nation, with the possible exception of some Nordic countries sometimes on some issues. In gendered light, given the empirical record, one wonders why international organizations were seen to raise questions of political representativeness that national organizations qua national seemingly did not. If this is backwards as to sex, perhaps it illuminates the lack of representativeness hence rationale for or legitimacy of the nation state, and calls for a questioning of its sovereignty on gendered terms, shedding new light on the potential of the international order and transnational governance where issues of inequality of sex are concerned.[10] Given women's increasing mobilization as such in international civil society, could women, in a unique transnational sense, be a people?

So he didn't do it all. He was always clear all was far from done. As he said with typical humility of *Democracy and Its Critics* (1989a), an effort of three decades, 'even that book raises nearly as many questions as it answers' (Dahl 1991, p. 293). Beyond his thin treatment of gender, even as its realities present sometimes major examples or thick counterexamples of the material he theorizes, Bob would want us to take up these questions, hammer, and tongs. This is a guy to whom women were real. Issues raised by women's status and treatment were not relegated to that box over there, as some other subject or isolated topic for some token

ROBERT A. DAHL

woman to pursue, but were central to the core questions of the politics he engaged, even if they could have been taken further.

It was our luck – mine in particular – that he was who he was. Opening doors to the future and setting us respectfully free on our own is how the true democrat, and one of the world's ten nicest men, prepared the way.

Disclosure statement

No potential conflict of interest was reported by the author.

Notes

1. My PhD. thesis became *Toward a Feminist Theory of the State* (MacKinnon 1989).
2. This locution is pervasive in his work but well-illustrated in *Toward Democracy* (Dahl 1997, p. 175) and 'Political Equality, Then and Now' (Dahl 2006b, p. 465).
3. One of his most engaging descriptions of this theme appears in *After The Revolution?* (Dahl 1970, p. 46).
4. See also *After the Revolution?* (Dahl 1970, pp. 64–65).
5. For his whole initial discussion, see pp. 5–15.
6. Rosaldo and Lamphere (1974), Draper (1975) and Leacock (1978) with the later Lee (1992) and the subsequent Guenther (2007) to the current McCall and Widerquist (2015).
7. For the systematic inadequacies of the Equal Protection Clause of the Fourteenth Amendment to women's unequal status and treatment, see *Sex Equality* (MacKinnon 2001/2007).
8. Literature from mainly the mid-1990s on gaining steam after 2000 is reviewed and discussed, e.g. Galligan (2006), Rodriguez-Ruiz and Rubio-Marin (2009) 'Gender parity is justified … as a democratic requirement', at p. 1195, Crook and Messing-Mathie (2013).
9. One example is *Democracy and Its Critics* (Dahl 1989a, p. 115).
10. For further exploration, see 'Women's Status, Men's States' (MacKinnon 2007).

References

Allen, A., 2010. Recognizing domination: recognition and power in Honneth's critical theory. *Journal of Power*, 3 (1), 21–32.

Butler, J., 1997. *The psychic life of power: theories in subjection*. Stanford, CA: Stanford University Press.

Crook, M.L. and Messing-Mathie, A., 2013. Gender quotas and comparative politics: past, present, and future research agendas. *Politics & Gender*, 9 (3), 299–303.

Dahl, R.A., 1940. *Socialist programs and democratic politics: an analysis*. Dissertation (PhD). Yale University.

ROBERT A. DAHL

Dahl, R.A., 1947. The science of public administration: three problems. *Public Administration Review*, 7 (1), 1–11.

Dahl, R.A., 1955. The science of politics: new and old. *World Politics*, 7 (3), 479–489 (review of David Easton, *The Political System: An Inquiry into the State of Political Science*, and Eric Voegelin, *The New Science of Politics: An Introductory Essay*).

Dahl, R.A., 1956. *A preface to democratic theory*. Berkeley: University of California Press.

Dahl, R.A., 1961. *Who governs? Democracy and power in an American city*. New Haven, CT: Yale University Press.

Dahl, R.A., 1963. *Modern political analysis*. Englewood Cliffs, NJ: Prentice-Hall.

Dahl, R.A., 1967. *Pluralist democracy in the United States: conflict and consent*. Chicago, IL: Rand McNally.

Dahl, R.A., 1970. *After the revolution? Authority in a good society*. New Haven, CT: Yale University Press.

Dahl, R.A., 1971. *Polyarchy: participation and opposition*. New Haven, CT: Yale University Press.

Dahl, R.A., 1980. Political equality and political rights. *Il Politico: Rivista Italiana di Scienze Politiche*, XLV (4), 557–570.

Dahl, R.A., 1985. *Controlling nuclear weapons: democracy versus guardianship*. Syracuse, NJ: Syracuse University Press.

Dahl, R.A., 1986. *Democracy, liberty and equality*. Oslo: Norwegian University Press.

Dahl, R.A., 1989a. *Democracy and its critics*. New Haven, CT: Yale University Press.

Dahl, R.A., 1989b. The pseudodemocratization of the American presidency. *In*: S. McMurrin, ed. *The Tanner lectures on human values* delivered at Harvard University, 11–12 April 1988. Cambridge: Cambridge University Press, 35–71.

Dahl, R.A., 1991. Reflections on a preface to democratic theory. *Government and Opposition*, 26 (3), 292–301.

Dahl, R.A., 1994. *The new American political (dis)order*. Berkeley: Institute of Governmental Studies Press.

Dahl, R.A., 1996. Equality versus inequality. *PS. Political Science & Politics*, 29 (4), 639–648.

Dahl, R.A., 1997. *Toward democracy – a journey: reflections, 1940–1997*. Berkeley: Institute of Governmental Studies Press.

Dahl, R.A., 1999. Can international organizations be democratic? A skeptic's view. *In*: I. Shapiro and C. Hacker-Cordon, eds. *Democracy's edges*. Cambridge: Cambridge University Press, 19–38.

Dahl, R.A., 2001. *How democratic is the American Constitution?* New Haven, CT: Yale University Press.

Dahl, R.A., 2002. For a more democratic union the sad fact is that the US Constitution falls woefully short of being the model document for a modern republic, a constitutional overhaul, within the framers' guidelines. *Boston Globe*, 21 July, p. D.1.

Dahl, R.A., 2005a. *After the gold rush: growing up in Skagway*. Philadelphia, PA: Xlibris.

Dahl, R.A., 2005b. What political institutions does large-scale democracy require? *Political Science Quarterly*, 120 (2), 187–197.

Dahl, R.A., 2006a. *On political equality*. New Haven, CT: Yale University Press.

Dahl, R.A., 2006b. Political equality, then and now. *The Tocqueville Review*, 27 (2), 461–475.

Dahl, R.A., 2006c. Reflections on human nature and politics: from genes to political institutions. *In*: L. Berman, ed. *The art of political leadership: essays in honor of Fred I. Greenstein*. New York: Rowman & Littlefield, 3–16.

Dahl, R.A. and Brown, R.S., Jr., 1951. *Domestic control of atomic energy*. New York: Social Science Research Council.

Dahl, R.A. and Lindblom, C.E., 1953. *Politics, economics, and welfare*. New York: Harper & Brothers.

Dahl, R.A. and Tufte, E.R., 1973. *Size and democracy*. Stanford, CA: Stanford University Press.

Draper, P., 1975. !Kung women: contrasts in sexual egalitarianism in foraging and sedentary contexts. *In*: R.R. Reiter, ed. *Toward an anthropology of women*. New York: Monthly Review Press, 77–109.

Galligan, Y., 2006. Bringing women in: global strategies for gender parity in political representation. *University of Maryland Law Journal of Race, Religion, Gender and Class*, 6 (2), 319–336.

Guenther, M., 2007. Current issues and future directions in hunter-gatherer studies. *Anthropos*, 102, 371–388.

Haugaard, M., 2012. Rethinking the four dimensions of power: domination and empowerment. *Journal of Political Power*, 5 (1), 33–54.

Lee, R.B., 1992. Art, science or politics? The crisis in hunter-gatherer studies. *American Anthropologist*, 94 (1), 31–54.

Leacock, E., 1978. Women's status in egalitarian society: implications for social evolution. *Current Anthropology*, 19 (2), 247–275.

Lukes, S., 1974. *Power: a radical view*. London: Macmillan.

MacKinnon, C.A., 1989. *Toward a feminist theory of the state*. Cambridge, MA: Harvard University Press.

MacKinnon, C.A., 2001/2007. *Sex equality*. New York: Foundation Press.

MacKinnon, C.A., 2007. Women's status, men's states. *In*: C.A. MacKinnon, ed. *Are women human?* Cambridge, MA: Harvard University Press, 1–16.

MacKinnon, C.A., 2012. Gender in world constitutions. *In*: M. Rosenfeld and A. Sajo, eds. *Handbook on comparative constitutional law*. Oxford: Oxford University Press, 418.

McCall, G.S. and Widerquist, K., 2015. The evolution of equality: rethinking variability and egalitarianism among modern forager societies. *Ethnoarchaeology*, 7 (1), 21–44.

Millett, K., 1969. *Sexual politics*. Garden City, NY: Doubleday.

Rosaldo, M.Z. and Lamphere, L., eds., 1974. *Woman, culture and society*. Stanford University Press.

Rodriguez-Ruiz, B. and Rubio-Marin, R., 2009. Constitutional justification of parity democracy. *Alabama Law Review*, 60 (5), 1171–1195.

Russell, D.E.H., 1983. The incidence and prevalence of intrafamilial and extrafamilial sexual abuse of female children. *Child Abuse & Neglect*, 7 (2), 133–146.

Robert Dahl on power

Steven Lukes

Department of Sociology, New York University, New York, NY, USA

Two questions about Dahl's evolving view of power are addressed. Have critics failed to distinguish his broad concept of power from the operational measures required for its study? It is argued that his classic study *Who Governs?* was driven by a concept of power on whose narrowness they rightly focused because it excluded important questions about power relations and mechanisms. Secondly, how satisfactory is his final conceptualization of power? This, it is argued, is still too narrow. It conflates power and influence, failing to see the importance of its dispositional character. It advances too narrow a view of its origins and its impact. And it fails to acknowledge the virtues of relating the concept of power to that of 'interests'.

Robert Dahl made truly major contributions to our understanding of democracy, as political theorist, political scientist, and critic. No less significant was his writing, extending across his career, about power, both analyzing the concept and deploying it in empirical research. I agree with Professor Stinebrickner that Dahl himself contributed to what he saw as 'the "vast improvement" in political and other social scientists' understanding of influence-terms' (Stinebrickner 2015, p. 194). That contribution was considerable and important, but it has, according to Professor Baldwin, been misunderstood and mischaracterized. It originated with the first of two articles on the concept of power in 1957 (Dahl 1957), to be followed by a second in 1968 (Dahl 1968), and continued with his sharply focused and salutary challenge to the 'ruling elite model' of C. Wright Mills (Dahl 1958) and with his major study of the distribution of power in New Haven, *Who Governs?* (Dahl 1961) and it culminated, after successive editions of his introductory text, *Modern Political Analysis* in the sixth edition of that work, published in 2003 (Dahl and Stinebrickner 2003), where we can read, in Stinebricnker's words, 'Dahl's last word in response to the many searching critics of his *Who Governs?*' (Stinebrickner 2015, p. 199) The publication together of Baldwin's and Stinebrickner's articles in this symposium offers a most welcome opportunity both to reconsider Dahl's developing views of power in light of the charge that they have been misinterpreted and to assess the strengths and weaknesses of his last word on this centrally important topic.

Misinterpreting Dahl

The gist of Baldwin's critique is that critics of Dahl on power failed 'to distinguish between the operational definition(s) of power used in *Who Governs?* and the abstract concept of power underlying it'. That abstract definition, set out in his 1957 article 'The concept of power', intended to capture 'the bedrock idea' and his 'intuitive idea of power', is: '*A* has power over *B* to the extent that he can get *B* to do something that *B* would not otherwise do' (Dahl 1957, pp. 202–203).

The first thing to notice about this definition is its extreme sparseness. It is almost devoid of content, conveying no more than the idea of a causal relation between two (presumably human) agents. That was, of course, its very point: Dahl's purpose, he wrote, was to 'catch the central intuitively understood meaning of the word' with a formal definition that explicates 'the primitive notion that seems to lie behind *all* of these concepts', such as power, influence, control, and authority (Dahl 1957, p. 202). It is, therefore, unsurprising that, as Baldwin notes, Dahl's abstract concept is 'broad enough to include changing *B*'s behavior by controlling agendas or suppressing issues as well as affecting *B*'s behavior by manipulating his consciousness' (Baldwin 2015, p. 222). It is also compatible with zero- and positive-sum power, direct and indirect, visible and invisible, unsubtle and subtle influence, and the use of material and non-material resources. Dahl himself obviously became dissatisfied with the excessive breadth of this early definition. It clearly failed to identify his own intuitive idea of power; hence, his successive revisions of the abstract concept culminating in his last word, to be considered below. It is broad enough to be compatible with literally innumerable other causal relations between agents that it would be counter-intuitive to view as cases of power. On this definition, for instance, I am powerful if I cause an accident that harms you, or if I lose a bet that makes you rich or if, because I bought the last ticket, you fail to see a movie. Indeed every modification of behavior (itself undefined) resulting from the actions or inaction of another or others falls under its scope. Dahl was himself obviously dissatisfied with the excessive breadth of this early definition. It clearly failed to identify his own intuitive idea of power; hence, his successive revisions of the abstract concept culminating in his last word, to be considered below. It is, in short, so broad that it fails to capture the 'central intuitively understood meaning' of 'power': what interests us when we as laymen discuss and as social scientists conduct research into the location, distribution, extent, and effects of power.

That is what we require from a concept of power: a guide to questions and an orientation for research. What are we looking for and how are we to recognize it? Thus, an adequate concept of power also, as Dahl himself insightfully observed, has the role of guiding researchers to appropriate operational measures or criteria, so that, if these are defective, 'at least we shall know they are defective and in what ways' (Dahl 1957, p. 214). The critics of *Who Governs?*, including the present writer, were in search of such a concept, but they did not find it in the 1957 definition. This was neither helpful in understanding the book's findings nor promising as a basis for future research into power. For the reasons indicated, the 'bedrock idea' supposedly 'underlying' the book could not provide adequate foundations for research. Baldwin writes that the critics would have been better advised 'to base observations about Dahl's concept of power on sources in which he actually discusses the concept' (Baldwin 2015, p. 222). But to do so would have been little help, since it is a very narrow construal of the 1957 definition that oriented the New Haven research and motivated its questions and much of the subsequent so-called 'community power debate' consisted in establishing that narrowness and broadening the questions.

ROBERT A. DAHL

The concept that actually drove the research of *Who Governs?* was shaped by two preconceptions that Dahl brought to his inquiries. One arose from doubts about the existing state of research. Dahl held that previous studies of power, both at the national and local level, had failed to address the question of *power comparability*. He questioned the portrayal of the distribution of power by both C. Wright Mills and Floyd Hunter as elite rule. In order to test such claims, one needed to discover which leaders prevailed over different kinds of issues. Criticizing Hunter and anticipating the research strategy of *Who Governs?* he asked:

> Are we to conclude that in 'Regional City' there is a small determinate group of leaders whose power significantly exceeds that of all other members of the community on all or many of the key issues that arise? Or are we to conclude, at the other extreme, that some leaders are relatively powerful on some issues and not on others, and that no leaders are relatively powerful on all issues? We have no way of choosing between these two interpretations or indeed among many others that might be formulated. (Dahl 1957, p. 208)

The second preconception was an assumption about the nature of politics in New Haven: the assumption that the city was a pluralist democracy in which there is a small number of active citizens with much direct influence on decisions, assisted by a corps of auxiliaries or subleaders; these leaders 'differ from area to area and disagree among themselves, and ... because of their disagreement they actively seek for support from constituents', who in turn exercise 'a moderate degree of indirect influence, for elected leaders keep the real or imagined preferences of constituents in mind in deciding what policies to adopt or reject' (Dahl 1961, pp. 102–103, 164–165). To test, or operationalize, this hypothesis and determine patterns of influence, the research needed to measure and compare the power or influence, direct and indirect, of leaders, subleaders, and constituents in decision-making by the city authorities over policies in respect of selected key issues. The method involved arriving at 'influence rankings' by studying decision-making in three key issue areas of New Haven political life.

What I have just briefly summarized is very well known to those familiar with this debate, but I have done so in order to illustrate the point that the concept of power/influence driving the research resulting in *Who Governs?* was not the broad 1957 concept, though it was, obviously, compatible with it. Power, as conceived by Dahl in 1961, was presented as distributed pluralistically among leaders, subleaders, and constituents in New Haven. It was the power to influence (that is, to prevail on the winning side) in policy-making on the part of participants where there was disagreement or conflict. This was operationalized by determining

> for each decision which participants had initiated alternatives that were finally adopted, had vetoed alternatives initiated by others, or had proposed alternatives that were turned down. These actions were then tabulated as individual 'successes' or 'defeats'. The participants with the greatest proportion of successes out of the total number of successes were then considered to be the most influential. (Dahl 1961, p. 330)

Power thus conceived is, self-evidently, of central importance in democratic politics, but, as Dahl's critics went on to argue and as Dahl himself obviously conceded, it offers an extremely limited view of power. There are other ways, including agenda control, the suppression of potential issues, the shaping of beliefs and preferences, and much else besides, in which power is at work in social and

ROBERT A. DAHL

political life that this way of conceiving it (that is, this concept) could not capture. *Who Governs?* is nevertheless a classic work of social scientific inquiry: a meticulous, thorough and indeed imaginative investigation of a precisely formulated object of study by means of appropriate operational measures. There is, I believe, no subsequent study of power that can be claimed as its equal in these respects.

Did the critics, then, misinterpret Dahl? Doubtless some have, and in various ways, and it is not my purpose to claim that none have. But I do want to conclude this section by discussing what lies behind Baldwin's defense of Dahl, which amounts to the claim that Dahl deployed his 1957 concept of power by operationalizing it in 1961. Thus, the critics are castigated for having frequently followed Bachrach and Baratz in supposing them to have 'identified a defect or limitation of Dahl's concept of power'. This, Baldwin writes, is misleading because, contrary to what they claimed they were doing,

> Bachrach and Baratz were criticizing the research methodology and one of the six operational measures used in *Who Governs?*, but this criticism has little to do with the abstract concept of power underlying the book and explicated in the 1957 article. (Baldwin 2015, p. 212)

Indeed those engaged in the subsequent debate believed they were disagreeing about the locus of community power but their disagreement was actually 'about methodology and operational measures, not about the abstract concept of power' (Baldwin 2015, p. 213). Dahl, in short, was being unfairly criticized for adopting a methodology and operational measures 'for purposes of a particular research project, i.e., a case study of influence in New Haven' (Baldwin 2015, p. 215).

The problem here is to clarify the distinction between a concept and an operational measure.[1] Let us say, as suggested above, that a concept identifies what you are looking for and an operational measure provides signs or indices or indicators by which you can recognize it. Following this suggestion, we can say that, in the absence of a discussion of the concept of power in the book and the unhelpfulness of the excessively broad 1957 definition, Dahl's critics were led to reconstruct, from a close reading of the text, the concept driving its research and informing its conclusions. In seeing it as overly narrow and in need of broadening, they were seeking to identify mechanisms of power and aspects of power relations that eluded that concept. Baldwin's case for the defense is that it was 'the research project, i.e. a case study of influence in New Haven', that dictated that narrowness. That is true only in the sense that it was the concept driving the research project that did so; but, the critics argued, there were further questions about power in New Haven and elsewhere that needed to be asked.

The last word

I have until now been following both Dahl and Baldwin in treating 'power' and 'influence' indiscriminately as equivalent in meaning and I shall argue below against doing so. I have also been following Baldwin in writing of Dahl's *abstract concept* of power. I now want to complicate the story by making two observations, which will suggest the need for a certain modification of vocabulary.

In the first place, we should recognize that there are degrees of abstraction: concepts can be more or less abstract. The problem with Dahl's 1957 concept was that it was too abstract to do the job required: namely, to capture what the various manifestations of power are manifestations of, what interests us when we are interested in power. The evolution in Dahl's thinking about this, helpfully traced by Stinebrickner, across the six editions of *Modern Political Analysis* show him to have been engaged in 'reconceptualization and rethinking in response to relevant scholarly work' so that the 'treatment of "forms of influence" ... seems to become increasingly systematic, instructive and penetrating in successive editions' of the book (Stinebrickner 2015, pp. 194, 196). This evolution was toward a less (though still) abstract conceptualization, toward one that captures recognizable and researchable power mechanisms and relations.

This leads to the second observation. This is that an abstract concept needs to be *interpreted* to be put to work. John Rawls calls such an interpretation a *conception*. Thus, he defines a *concept* of justice as 'a proper balance between competing claims' whereas a *conception* of justice provides 'a set of related principles for identifying the relevant considerations that determine this balance'. The role of the concept lies in 'assigning rights and duties and in defining the appropriate division of social justice' while '[a] conception of justice is an interpretation of this role' (Rawls 1999, p. 9). Rawls's own theory of justice as fairness is one such conception.

It is worth noting at this point that Rawls allows for a plurality of such conceptions, while, of course, arguing for the superiority of his own. This points to another debate that relates to the present discussion, namely, the debate over the so-called essential contestedness of concepts. If a concept, such as justice or power, can, it would seem, be interpreted in several incompatible ways, two questions arise. First, why not say that we just have a plurality of different concepts? In respect of power, Dahl himself firmly rejected this option in 1957, arguing, in the name of a 'conceptual theoretician' against an 'operationalist', that the concept of power does indeed have a 'pure meaning' (Dahl 1957, p. 214). Second, how are we to reconcile the recognition of divergent apparently defensible interpretations or conceptions with the claim that one is superior? The answer here, I suggest, is that the participants in such a debate are likely to apply differing criteria to the selection of the best interpretation, according a different priority or weight to the considerations in favor of each. Thus, one may claim that a certain conception allows one to see further and deeper into what is at issue, another may argue that an alternative conception is more respectful of the autonomy or responsibility of human agents, another may hold that a third conception is more accessible to empirical research, and so on.

Baldwin notes that in my book *Power: A Radical View* I make a distinction between a 'concept' and a 'view' and that in a 'cryptic footnote' I indicate that this is 'closely parallel' to Rawls's distinction between concept and conception. I hope that I have here rendered less cryptic what I meant. Views of power, in my terminology, are like conceptions in being contending defensible interpretations of a more abstract concept and susceptible to potentially unending and irresolvable contestation, for the reasons suggested. Thus, a view of power, in my lexicon, is not, as Baldwin suggests, equivalent to 'an "operational definition," "operational measure," and/or "empirical indicator"' (Baldwin 2015, p. 214), but rather an interpreted concept, for which such operational measures or indicators are required in research.

At this point, however, an exercise in *mea culpa* is in order. A certain path dependence was at work in the community power debate such that the participants

ROBERT A. DAHL

were focused on a conflict model in which the power of actors consists in prevailing over other actors, to the neglect of the innumerable ways in which power can be beneficial, collaborative, and empowering. This was pointed out by many subsequent contributors to the discussion. Thus, I plainly erred in proposing a concept of power 'according to which A exercises power over B when affects B in a manner contrary to B's interests' (Lukes 1974, pp. 27, 34). Dahl was entirely correct to write in 2003 that

> in excluding forms of influence by A that are *favorable* to B's interests, Lukes's definition is not only contrary to common usage in ordinary language, political science and political philosophy but seems rather arbitrary as well. By excluding all situations in which A's control is not contrary to B's interests, Lukes's definition arbitrarily leaves out cases that we might reasonably count as involving influence. (Dahl and Stinebrickner 2003, p. 15)

In this important respect, Dahl and Stinebrickner's (2003) definition is obviously an improvement on mine. But what are we to make of it overall? Does it succeed in encompassing conceptions or views of power that embrace the range of relationships and mechanisms in which we are interested when we think and talk about and research into power? Let us now turn to considering the definition at which Dahl finally, after much reflection, arrived:

> For us, then, influence can be defined as *a relation among human actors such that the wants, desires, preferences, or intentions of one or more actors affect the actions, or predispositions to act, of one or more actors in a direction consistent with – and not contrary to – the wants, preferences, or intentions of the influence-wielders.* (Dahl and Stinebrickner 2003, p. 17)

As Stinebrickner suggests, this definition, together with the subsequent discussion of 'forms of influence' (inducement and power, force and coercion, persuasion and manipulation, and authority) and the levels at which influence can be exercised (among available options, over agendas, over agenda-setting structures, and over consciousness) constitute the book's 'greatest analytical contributions' and go far in the direction of 'integrating the contributions of others with his own core insights … and presenting them in straightforward, commonsense language, together with examples that usefully illustrate conceptual and theoretical points' (Stinebrickner 2015, pp. 197, 201). But Dahl's last word could hardly be expected to be the last word on the topic. There are, indeed, several ways in which, on close inspection, it still appears too narrow and, to use Stinebrickner's term, insufficiently 'penetrating'.

The first is indicated by his explicit and deliberate conflation of power and influence. This dates from the beginning of Dahl's thinking about power and is present throughout: as he wrote in 1957,

> I should like to be permitted to use these terms interchangeably when it is convenient to do so, without denying or seeming to deny that for many other purposes distinctions are necessary and useful. (Dahl 1957, p. 202)

But this conflation is certainly at odds with the ordinary meanings of these terms. It is clear, as Peter Morriss has persuasively argued, that '"power" and "influence" do overlap, but that at their cores are very different ideas, and that therefore neither is a subcategory of the other or can be replaced by it'. Thus, '"power" always refers to a *capacity* to do things, whilst "influence" (and typically) does not'. 'Power', in short, 'is always a concept referring to an ability, capacity or dispositional property' and indeed a power 'is a disposition that may or may not be activated' (Morriss 2002, pp. 12, 13, 24). Dahl's entire approach, however, focuses on causal influence: as he writes,

> It is this very sphere of human activity – influence by a person or a group of persons over the actions of dispositions of another person or group of persons – that constitutes the focus of modern political analysis as we know it. (Dahl and Stinebrickner 2003, p. 13)

Indeed, Dahl writes, 'For us, then, **politics** is simply *the exercise of influence*' (Dahl and Stinebrickner 2003, p. 24).

This conflation of terms matters because, according to Dahl's definition of *influence*, we are to attend only to actual affecting – or to use the language of power, to the *exercise* of power – rather than to its possession. Thus, our attention is deflected from the significance of power as a disposition – as ability or capacity (that may not need to be actualized) and thus from power relationships, for instance in countless hierarchical settings, where social status is enough to generate deference or compliance without any affecting being enacted by 'influence-wielders' (though often, of course, it will be). Power, to be effective and significant, does not always need to be 'wielded', and certainly not all the time. (Indeed, the very phrase 'influence-wielder' is revealing, since it excludes the effects of inaction). It is true that Dahl devotes some pages to the discussion of 'indirect influence' in *Who Governs?* in relation to the role of elections, but this does not meet the need to address the role of power in social and political life independently of its exercise.

In fact, confusingly, Dahl *does* distinguish influence from power, but only at the point where he is discussing the 'forms of influence'. Here power is treated, not as a dispositional property, but rather, in contrast with inducement, as the use of threats to secure compliance. Thus

> power occurs when B does what A wants because A will deprive B of something B values unless B complies with A's wishes. In other words, power is at work when compliance is attained by creating the prospect of severe sanctions for noncompliance. (Dahl and Stinebrickner 2003, p. 38)

This is, actually, doubly confusing, since we end up with two meanings of 'power' – one as equivalent to 'influence' and the other as a distinctive form of it; and secondly because the latter is not clearly distinct from another form of influence distinguished by Dahl, namely 'coercion', except insofar as coercion involves the even more severe sanction of a threatened use of force.

A second way in which Dahl's definition is insufficiently broad and deep concerns its characterization of the *cause* where influence is at work or power being exercised (or wielded): namely, 'the wants, desires, preferences, or intentions of one or more actors'. In the first place, as we have just seen, power may, in any case, not need to be exercised to be effective and significant, for instance as social status: it does not need to be *enacted*. Likewise, it does not need to be *experienced* by the powerful, in the form of 'wants, desires, preferences, or intentions'. I can have power over you without realizing or even caring about it. But that is also true of power when it is exercised or enacted. Routine administrative decisions by powerful officials and buying and selling decisions by powerful investors can have all kinds of unforeseen consequences. And indeed often actions of the powerful are mainly, even entirely, driven by roles and norms with consequences of which they are unaware, as when managers of corporations take decisions with economic consequences that may, or may not, benefit the corporation but not, at least directly, themselves. Indeed, is there not something odd, given Dahl's behaviorism, in the definition's attributing a causal role to subjective states, such as 'wants, desires, preferences, or intentions'?

A third limitation of the definition concerns the *effects* of power's exercise. In 1957, these were confined to the modification by A of B's *behavior*. In successive editions of *Modern Political Analysis*, this was extended to 'actions or predispositions to act' of those affected or influenced by the powerful. This extension is, clearly, an advance toward greater depth, or 'penetration', in the analysis of relations and mechanisms of power, for it allows consideration of the impact of the powerful on beliefs, emotions, experience, character, tastes, and what Pierre Bourdieu calls *habitus*. But this still leaves aside, and indeed deflects attention from, what must surely count as an often far more important way in which the power of the powerful has an impact on people's lives, namely its impact on their *circumstances*. Obviously, these will in turn affect their behavior and predispositions, but the focus of the definition on the latter fails to address the fact that often it is, and should be, the former that is of primary concern.

I turn, finally, to an issue that Dahl himself addressed under the subheading 'Interests versus Desires'. We are typically concerned, Dahl observes, in political analysis with 'results favorable or positive for the actor exerting influence' (or, to be precise, according to the last iteration of the definition, those that are not unfavorable). But how are we to determine this: by discovering that an outcome corresponds to the actor's 'desires or preferences' or, in Dahl's words, by reference to something 'more substantial and consequential for human beings than desires or preferences'? He decides against the latter course on the ground that

> just as with influence and related terms like power, 'interest' has also proved to be extraordinarily difficult to define, at least in any way that manages to avoid highly controversial judgments in a great many concrete cases.

Thus, for example, in reference to John Gaventa's study of Appalachian miners (Gaventa 1982), the mine owners, along with state and Federal officials, prevented the miners from gaining recognition of the mine-workers union. But, depending on one's theoretical assumptions, it is disputable whose interests this prevention served, for

> in order to judge whether a union was in the interests of the miners, or its prevention was in the interests of the owners, we need a theory of interests, both short-run and long-run. We happen to share with many others a theory (loose though it may be) from which we conclude that a union was in the interests of the miners, and very likely in the long-run interests of the owners as well. But this is a highly contestable theory. (Dahl and Stinebrickner 2003, pp. 15, 16)

In tying power to intentions (and the associated phenomena, 'wants, desires and preferences') Dahl joins a venerable tradition of thinkers who have written and thought seriously about power from Max Weber and Bertrand Russell onwards. It certainly comes naturally to us to think of exercising power, with Weber, as realizing one's will or, with Russell, as producing intended effects. But when, whether as laymen or researchers, we ask questions about power – about which individuals and categories of people have more or less power over which others and with what effects – our concern extends beyond the actual intentions of individuals, which, as we have seen, will often be at variance with and irrelevant to both the meaning and the effects of their power. And the inadequacy of seeing power as realizing intentions of individuals becomes all the clearer when we consider issues of collective power – of the power of states, organizations, institutions, corporations, coalitions, classes, social movements and the like. Thus, for example, understanding the specific intentions of specific mine owners and state and Federal officials, in the example just cited, is irrelevant to understanding what they were doing and to assessing its effects. (Suppose, for example, that, albeit improbably, they, or some of them, misunderstood what they were doing, believing, say, that they were facilitating the miners' union, they would still have been doing the same thing).

What, then, of Dahl's objection to enlisting the concept of 'interests' in explicating the concept of power? His objection was that the term is difficult to define and 'strongly theory-dependent' and 'theories about human interests are among the most controversial in philosophy, political science and social theory' (Dahl and Stinebrickner 2003, p. 16). But if the concept of interests is needed in clarifying and extending our understanding of power and power relations, then these difficulties may just have to be faced. One can, after all, account for power relations in the case of the Appalachian miner owners, in the manner Dahl sketches, by indicating, as he does, from what theory of interests one is making one's argument. What, I believe, renders the concept of interests valuable is its very *versatility*. It indicates *what matters*, or is advantageous, to people, whether as individuals, as human beings, as occupants of roles or as members of groups or other collectivities, and it can do so in a variety of ways. People have multiple interests, in these various capacities, some of which conflict. Their interests may be viewed as subjective or objective. If the former, they can range from passing whims to long-term life projects. (It is unclear what Dahl's point was in distinguishing wants, desires, preferences and intentions). If objective, interests can take various forms. They can, for instance, signify needs (as in a single mother's interest in child care), role requirements (as in a military officer's interest in his soldiers' obeying orders), competitive advantage (as in a state's military victory or a company's winning a bid), or the conditions for adequate human functioning (such as health and sufficient nutrition). There is thus a wide variety of ways in which power may be said to bring about 'results favorable or positive [or, on the latest version not unfavorable or negative] for the actor exerting influence'. Surveying this range, we can see how the concept of interests allows us to pinpoint conflicts among multiple interests, both between subjective interests and between subjective and objective interests. (Thus, for example, satisfying my taste for ice cream may both quench my appetite and subvert my dieting and thus my health). My point is that, in singling out 'wants, desires, preferences, or intentions', Dahl's definition takes interests to be subjective but in a way that (1) does not help us to distinguish different kinds of subjective interest and (2) is unduly restrictive in excluding objective interests.

This enables us to see how invoking interests in order to understand power relations enables us to perceive a kind of power relationship and mechanism, the

ROBERT A. DAHL

possibility, and researchability, of which Dahl does not (so far as I know) consider, though others, including his collaborator and expositor Nelson Polsby (see Polsby 1980), strongly deny: namely, that which involves the shaping by some of the subjective beliefs and interests (wants, desires, and preferences) of others in ways that harm or subvert their objective interests (see Lukes 2011). But that is another story, and another debate.

Conclusion

This article addresses two questions concerning Robert Dahl's evolving views about the concept of power, about which he wrote in two articles and in successive editions of his *Modern Political Analysis* and which he deployed in his magisterial study of politics in New Haven, *Who Governs?*

The first question is exegetical: have Dahl's critics, including the present writer, misinterpreted him, by failing to distinguish the concept of power from the methodology or operational measures required for its study, thus failing to see that *Who Governs?* deploys Dahl's earliest account of the concept of power? In response, that account is shown to be far too broad and sparse to have guided the research reported in the book. Instead, this was, as we have seen, driven by a concept of power on whose narrowness the critics rightly focused, on the grounds that it excluded a range of important questions about power relations and mechanisms that needed to be asked.

The second question addresses those questions. Remarkably and to his great credit, Dahl himself addressed them, broadening and deepening his definition of the concept of power across successive editions of *Modern Political Analysis*. But the definition at which he finally arrived is, we have argued, still too narrow in several important respects, failing to capture aspects of power relations and mechanisms in which we are interested when we ask questions about power. By conflating power and influence, it fails to see power as dispositional and thus not needing to be activated to have significant effects. Supposing that power must by definition express the intentions of the powerful, this account misses routine and unconsidered power and the unintended consequences of following roles and norms, and it fails to account for the power of collectives, such as states, institutions, and social movements. In claiming that the impact of power must be upon others' 'actions or dispositions to act', the definition neglects its impact on their circumstances. And in tying power to individuals' intentions, it fails to acknowledge the virtues of tying it to the concept of 'interests', the chief virtue of which is to reveal that conflict can occur between our interests and that power can be at work in generating it.

Disclosure statement

No potential conflict of interest was reported by the author.

Note

1. That both Dahl and Baldwin may have been unsure or even confused about this distinction is suggested by Baldwin's footnote 7, which reads: 'The terms operational definition and operational measure are often used interchangeably'.

References

Baldwin, D.A., 2015. Misinterpreting Dahl. *Journal of Political Power*, 8 (2), 209–227.

Dahl, R.A., 1957. The concept of power. *Behavioral Science*, 2 (3), 201–215.

Dahl, R.A., 1958. A critique of the ruling elite model. *American Political Science Review*, 52 (2), 263–469.

Dahl, R.A., 1961. *Who governs?*. New Haven, CT: Yale University Press.

Dahl, R.A., 1968. Power. In: David L. Sills, ed. *International encyclopedia of the social sciences*. New York, NY: Free Press, 405–415.

Dahl, R.A. and Stinebrickner, B., 2003. *Modern political analysis*. Upper Saddle River, NJ: Prentice-Hall.

Gaventa, J., 1982. *Power and powerlessness: quiescence and rebellion in an Appalachian valley*. Champaign, IL: University of Illinois Press.

Lukes, S., 1974. *Power: a radical view*. London: Macmillan.

Lukes, S., 2011. In defense of 'false consciousness'. *University of Chicago Legal Form for 2011*, 19–28.

Morriss, P., 2002. *Power: a philosophical analysis*. 2nd ed. Manchester, NH: Manchester University Press.

Polsby, N.W., 1980. *Community power and political theory*. Second enlarged ed. New Haven, CT: Yale University Press.

Rawls, J., 1999. *A theory of justice*. Revised ed. Cambridge, MA: The Belknap Press of Harvard University Press.

Stinebrickner, B., 2015. Robert A. Dahl and the essentials of *Modern Political Analysis*: politics, influence, power, and polyarchy. *Journal of Political Power*, 8 (2), 189–207.

Dahl's power and republican freedom

Philip Pettit

Princeton University

Dahl's classic analysis of power needs a few more or less minor corrections and it needs to be extended so that power can be exercised other than by punctual actions and can have other than punctual effects. But corrected and extended in this way, it provides a base from which it is possible to articulate a number of radical points of view and, in particular, to define the sort of control or domination that is opposed to freedom, on the traditional republican conception.

Introduction

Robert Dahl's classic discussion of the power of one party over another remains of relevance and importance in contemporary political theory, despite all the commentary and criticism to which it has been subjected (Dahl 1957). This paper tries to support that claim by showing how his analysis, suitably regimented, can serve in the articulation of the concept of freedom associated with the long republican tradition (Pettit 1997, Skinner 1998, Richardson 2002, Viroli 2002, Maynor 2003, Pettit 2007). According to this way of viewing things, the antonym of freedom is not interference but the power associated with being able to exercise interference, in particular arbitrary interference. Dahl's concept of power points us towards a very effective way of spelling out that view.

My paper is in three sections. First, I argue that there are some fine-grained revisions that Dahl's analysis needs; this discussion is slightly technical and some readers may prefer to skip it. Second, I argue that the amended Dahlian analysis can be usefully extended beyond the paradigm case on which he focuses, where punctual targets and tactics are involved. Third, I show that there are two important distinctions to be made within the emerging category of power or control and that, with those distinctions made, the category enables us to define republican freedom. The distinctions are between congenial and uncongenial forms of control and between controlled and uncontrolled, or non-arbitrary and arbitrary, versions of uncongenial control. According to the analysis presented, someone will be free in a given choice to the extent that no one exercises uncongenial, uncontrolled control over that choice.

Before proceeding, one preliminary matter. Dahl's conceptualization allows for a distinction between possessing and exercising power. To possess power over another will be to have access to the resources that allow one to affect the behavior of another; to exercise power will be to make use of those resources for that purpose. I shall often make use of that distinction in what follows, although Dahl does not explicitly mark it in his original analysis (but see Dahl 2002).

1. Amending Dahl's analysis

Dahl concentrates on the case where A, drawing on a base of available resources, adopts a discrete or punctual means in order to exercise control over a discrete or punctual response on the part of

ROBERT A. DAHL

B (Dahl 1957). The focus is the 'mediating activity by A between A's base and B's response' (p. 203). The paradigm case is one where A, by doing something w to B, exercises power over whether B does x shortly after.

Critics might reject Dahl's concentration on the case where one party exercises power over another, rather than cases of power more generally; for an overview of more general issues, see (Dahl 2002). That looks like criticizing him for having dealt with the wrong question, however, rather than criticizing him for having dealt badly with the question addressed. He should not be taken to be trying to analyze power in general, only the power exercised by one party over another (Morriss 2002). I shall have nothing more to say about this line of criticism, though I do comment on the related complaint that it is less than fully satisfactory to focus just on punctual tactics – A's action, w – in order to affect a punctual target: B's action, x.

Dahl's core idea about the paradigm case can be stated very briefly. A has or possesses power over B's x-ing to the extent that B can do w and, by doing w, raise the probability that B x's. The increase in probability level gives the measure of A's power. Dahl's central idea is on target, I believe, but there are three ways in which he goes amiss in commenting on it and developing it.

The first slip occurs in the comment that he casually makes on the paradigm, when he says that where the idea applies, A 'can get B to do something that B would not otherwise do' (p. 203). This is an incautious and mistaken gloss, at least on face-value interpretation. For A can raise the probability that B x's by w-ing, and can thereby exercise power over B, even if it happens that B would have done x in any case. A can exercise power without leading B to do something B would not otherwise have done. Suppose you are going to attend a meeting of your own inclination but that I take an action that increases the probability of your being there, say because it guards against a change of mind on your part. I will exercise power over you in doing this, even though I do not make you do something you would not otherwise have done.

The second slip that Dahl makes comes in his account of the baseline by reference to which we determine whether A makes it more probable that B x's. To say that by taking action w, A makes it more probable that B x's invites the question: more probable than what? Dahl's answer is: more probable than B's x-ing would have been in the absence of A's action, w. But that answer is not completely satisfactory.

Suppose that B is affected just by the fact that A is present in B's life so that no matter what A does, no matter even if A omits to do anything, A's presence reduces the probability that B will x; it reduces that probability below the level that it would have been at, had A not made an appearance at all. It would be paradoxical in such a situation to say that there is something A can do to exercise power over whether B x's. A is worse than powerless in relation to B's x-ing, say because A triggers defiance in B, as an intrusive parent might trigger defiance in a teenager. A makes it more probable that B will not x than it would have been had A not been in the picture: had A been absent or inattentive. In that situation, however, it may well be the case that by taking the action, w – say, by apologizing for intruding – A raises the probability of B's x-ing above the level it would have if A had not taken that action. So on Dahl's analysis A has or possesses power over whether A x's.

The lesson of this observation is straightforward, though it may not have importance in many practical cases. We should say that by taking action w, A exercises power over whether B x's only if A thereby raises the probability that B x's beyond the level it would have had in A's absence. It is not enough that A raises the probability beyond the level it would have had just in the absence of A's taking action w. A's taking action w may be an attempt to make the best of a bad lot, not anything we would want to think as an exercise of power.

ROBERT A. DAHL

Now to the third problem with Dahl's analysis of the paradigm case. In explicating the idea that A raises the probability that B x's, Dahl invokes the notion of conditional probability. He does so when he takes (a) and (b) as equivalent:

(a) by doing w, A raises the probability that B x's;
(b) the probability of B's x-ing, given that A does w, is higher than the probability of B's x-ing, given that A does not do w.

However (a) and (b) are not equivalent. Suppose that A and B are friends. The probability that B is in hospital, given that A sends B flowers, is higher than the probability that B is in hospital, given that A does not send B flowers. Nevertheless, A's sending B flowers is a sign of B's having gone to hospital, not the source of that move. A does not raise the probability of B being in hospital – not, in the intended, practical sense of that phrase – by sending B flowers and there is no question of A's exercising power over B.

In order for A to raise the probability that B x's, by doing w, A's action must make the probability rise, not just show that it has risen. This is best explicated by the probability attaching to the conditional 'If A should do w, B would x', not by the conditional probability of B's x-ing, given that A does w. The point will be familiar from the arguments in favor of causal over evidential decision theory (Joyce 1999). But this is not the place to pursue that rival explication; I am content just to note that some such amendment is necessary.

2. Extending Dahl's analysis

Beyond punctual tactics and targets

Dahl's account of the power of one party over another can be extended so that it does not require the power-holder to perform a punctual action, w, with a view to having an effect on a punctual action, x; these variables, 'x' and 'w', can be allowed to range over a wider domain. The attraction of the extension is that it enables the account to escape a number of influential critiques, and to make sense of the fact that one party can exercise power over another without actually doing anything at all.

Following this strategy, we fix the actors involved in a power relation, be they individuals or groups or organizations, but do not require the means available or the response targeted to be punctual in character. We put no restriction on the means or tactics whereby power is exercised and allow the response targeted to be a discrete response, a general disposition, a habit of thought, or a mind-set. This extended account of power may reduce the operational applicability of the idea, making it too complex to support a simple index or set of indices. However, it has two distinct advantages.

First advantage

First, the departure enables the account to allow for at least a number of cases where power is possessed and exercised in virtue of agenda-fixing or attitude-shaping resources (Bachrach and Baratz 1962, Lukes 1974). There is no block to including extended resources in the arsenal of power, once the exercise of power is not associated with punctual means that are directed at punctual responses. Thus there is no reason why A's power should not affect what B does at a given time, or over time, in virtue of initiatives taken earlier or over time; no reason why it should not be exercised over someone in virtue of general initiatives that are not directed at that individual in particular; no reason why the initiatives should not go behind the back of the individual and rig his or her motives or mind-set; and so on. The extended, Dahlian notion looks quite capable of handling a variety of such cases.

118

ROBERT A. DAHL

Second advantage

The second advantage of extending Dahl's analysis beyond punctual tactics and punctual targets is that it makes it possible to see that A may exercise power over B's x-ing – this may continue to be taken as a punctual action – even in cases where A does not interfere in any positive way with B; even where B does nothing (Pettit 1997). The broadened concept of power allows us to see that power may be exercised even in cases where there is no active interference.

A may interfere to raise the probability that B x's in any of a variety of ways. Under each variation, A worsens B's choice-situation. B may be deprived of certain resources, executive or informational, or may have certain options removed or replaced by inferior alternatives. The salient possibilities are these:

- A manipulates B's mind-set, thereby reducing B's capacity for deliberation;
- A imposes a sure or probabilistic block, real and/or purported, on B's not x-ing;
- A imposes a sure or probabilistic burden, real and/or purported, on B's not x-ing
- A misinforms B about the blocks and burdens in place, to get B to x.

In each of these cases it is plausible that A exercises power over B in the choice of x. However, it turns out that A may exercise such power over B without interfering actively at all.

Suppose that A has preferences over how B behaves in a given type of situation, though preferences that may in principle vary from time to time. Imagine that A does not in general interfere with B in that situation, finding what B does acceptable – perhaps even finding it acceptable on some occasions that B should behave in whatever way B wishes. But suppose that A is poised to interfere, should B make a choice that turns out not to appeal to A; suppose A interferes with B, only on a need-for-interference basis, where the need is dictated by A's preferences at the time. In such a case, we may say that A invigilates B's choice, interfering only when the choice does not please. A's invigilation may not be a conscious or intentional action that would provide a referent for 'w' in the original schema; it may consist merely in being there, ready to interfere – and interfere intentionally – should B not behave to A's taste.

Does A exercise power over B's choice, and do so both in the cases where interference is triggered, and in the cases where it is not? Yes, on the extended Dahlian analysis, A exercises power over B even in the absence of actual interference. Take the case where B is disposed to act in a way that pleases A. Even in such a case, A's invigilation of B raises the probability that B will indeed act in that way; it guards against a change of mind on B's part. A will exercise power over B just in virtue of invigilating B. Whatever B does will be done, more or less implicitly, by A's leave; B, in the old republican phrase, will act only *cum permissu*, only with permission.[1]

It will be true that A exercises power over B in such a case, whether or not B becomes aware of A's invigilating presence and A's capacity to interfere. However, if B becomes aware of A's presence and potential – or indeed if B mistakenly ascribes a potentially effective, invigilating presence to A – then A's exercise of power will run on an independent motor. If B seeks not to trigger A's interference, B may second-guess A's wishes and seek to keep A happy. B may self-censor his or her choices with a view to placating A or even resort to attempts at self-ingratiation. At this limit, A exercises the most exquisite form of power over B: a form of power in which B is both the mediator of A's control and its victim. Not only does A invigilate B, thereby helping to ensure that B acts as required; A inhibits or intimidates B, thereby making this assurance doubly assured.

3. From power to freedom

Amending and extending Dahl's analysis of power takes us to the borders of normative theory. Let one person exercise power over another's choice, on the pattern of that analysis – let one

ROBERT A. DAHL

person have a degree of control over the other's choice – and the natural question to ask is whether the person affected suffers a reduction of freedom in that choice. I argue, in line with the republican tradition, that such control involves a loss of freedom, provided it is uncongenial rather than congenial, and uncontrolled rather than controlled. It will be useful in conclusion, then, if I show how these distinctions apply within the amended and extended analysis.

Congenial and uncongenial control

In order to deliberate about what to do, in the manner that is distinctive of human beings, we have to assume with respect to the options before us in any context that we can take one or we can take another; call this the principle of personal choice. The principle holds that in any such choice the options are there for us as things that, in the most basic sense possible, are available for choice. Sometimes, of course, we think of an option, not in the basic terms in which it is so available, but under the richer description that reaches out to include a desired but uncertain consequence; we think of it as hitting the target, for example, rather than just trying to hit the target. However, in every case of deliberation and decision there has to be an aspect under which each option presents itself to us such that we can think: I can do that or not do that; whether I do it, is up to me.[2]

With the notion of personal choice explained, it is possible to distinguish between congenial and uncongenial exercises of power: congenial and uncongenial forms of control. Suppose that B faces a personal choice between options x, y and z and that A exercises power in raising the probability that B will do x, whether on a particular occasion or more generally. This exercise of power will be congenial if it leaves the can-do assumption in place with each option; if it enables B to think, and think correctly, of each option as it was originally presented, I can just do that or not do that; it is up to me. The exercise of power will be uncongenial, on the other hand, if it undermines or jeopardizes this assumption in the case of any of the options.

The congenial exercise of power is associated with reasoning or deliberation. As human beings reason with themselves, shaping their own deliberation and decision-making, so they can play this same reasoning role, not just with themselves, but also with one another. They can lend one another their reason, as it were, taking the part of advisors or collaborators, and helping one another to get clear on the options available in any choice and on the pros and cons of those alternatives. They can act in relation to one another as an *amicus curiae*, a friend of the court. This will show up particularly in the fact that the help provided in such co-reasoning, like the help provided in self-reasoning, leaves the agent in a position to choose as he or she will; the advice or analysis provided may be rejected.

A may exercise a degree of control over B via co-reasoning or deliberation of this kind, changing the probabilities attached to one or more of the options that are thought to be available. Nevertheless, that sort of control will not be uncongenial, since it will do nothing to undermine the can-do assumptions associated with personal choice. Where B could rightly have made a can-do assumption prior to receiving counsel, he or she will still be able to endorse that assumption in its wake. The claim that co-reasoning is a congenial exercise of power will be unsurprising but it supports a corresponding line on the rather more controversial case, where one agent controls what another does by making an offer rather than issuing a threat (Nozick 1969). The line supported is that normal offers or rewards do not make for an uncongenial form of control.

Suppose that A is deliberating with B about what B should do, as in the model just given of congenial control. One of the things that A may usefully point out to B, and do so without exercising uncongenial control, is that the options available, say x, y, and z, can be extended to include the option of choosing y and getting a reward from C for doing so. This will be so if C really wants B to take x, and might be prepared, at least if approached in advance, to promise to reward the choice of that option. Now suppose that what is true of C under this hypothesis is

ROBERT A. DAHL

actually true of A, and that A knows this. And suppose that A points out to B that as a matter of fact there is a further option available, apart from x, y and z, neat; this is the option, x+, of doing x and receiving a reward from A for doing so. If A's telling B about C was not an instance of uncongenial control, neither can A's telling B about A – thereby effectively making an offer – be an instance of uncongenial control. It will not be an instance of uncongenial control so long as the offer is refusable, sincere, and non-mesmerizing.

By contrast with the deliberative case – including the case of a regular, refusable offer – A's control over B's choice will be uncongenial to the extent that it manipulates B's capacity to choose deliberatively or undermines the truth or the thinkability of one of B's correct can-do assumptions. The control exercised may undermine the truth of an assumption by removing one option from the set of options available, as in rendering the choice of that option impossible. Alternatively, it may undermine the truth of an assumption by replacing that option by one that involves an extra difficulty or penalty or constraint (or perhaps an extra, unrefusable reward); with such a rider attached to an option, B will no longer be able to think rightly of the option, as originally presented: I can do *that*. Alternatively, finally, the control exercised by A may undermine the thinkability of a can-do assumption by leading B to believe – rightly or wrongly – that one or another of the options has been removed or replaced.

How might A exercise uncongenial control over B? There are a number of possibilities, as already registered in the second section.

- *Interference*. A may interfere with B in manipulating B's choice, in removing or replacing an option, or in deceiving B about the options available.
- *Invigilation*. With or without B's awareness, A may stand by and invigilate B's choice for whether it is, or is likely to be, to A's taste; let it be acceptable and A does nothing, let it be unacceptable and A interferes.
- *Inhibition*. A may inhibit B by inducing or availing of a belief in B, mistaken or otherwise, that A is able to interfere in those ways. This may lead B to exercise self-censorship or self-ingratiation: to try to avoid choices that are displeasing to A or to try to give A an incentive not to practice interference.[3]

These different varieties of impact will involve uncongenial control, since they all undermine the deliberative assumption of personal choice; this is the assumption that with each option originally on offer the agent, B, is positioned to think, and rightly think, I can just do that. Interference does this by its very definition. Invigilation does it insofar as it replaces an option – perhaps every single option in the choice – by a burdened substitute: an option, z, will be replaced by z-provided-it-is-to-A's-taste. And inhibition does it insofar as B takes A, rightly or wrongly, to have replaced an option in that manner; where B could previously see z as an available option, for example, the option presented will now be: z-provided-it-is-to-A's-taste.[4]

Controlled and uncontrolled control

With the category of uncongenial control defined, it may seem that we can say: a person is free in a given choice just to the extent that no one exercises uncongenial control over the choice. That is not quite right, according to the republican tradition. For the tradition always makes a point of stressing that what is important is that no one exercise uncongenial control on an arbitrary rather than a non-arbitrary basis.[5]

This distinction is not spelled out very carefully in the long republican tradition but I have suggested elsewhere that it may plausibly be taken as the distinction between control, on the one hand, that is not forced to track the interests that the controlled person is disposed to avow – not forced to track the person's interests according to his or her own judgments – and control, on the other hand, that is restricted by being forced to track those interests (Pettit 1997). Moreover, understood in that way, we can make good sense of the distinction within the broad terms with which we have been working here.

Suppose that I am worried about smoking too much and decide to ask my partner to keep the key to the tobacco box hidden and to refuse to give it to me before dinnertime. Suppose, in particular, that this regime is subject to my continuing affirmation; I can withdraw at dinnertime on any day by calling it off for later periods. In the scenario envisaged, I am subject to the uncongenial control of my partner during daytime, since the option of having a smoke is removed from me, or at least made somewhat more difficult. However, intuitively, this sort of control is not a violation of my freedom, since the regime that allows it is subject to my own continuing control. My partner's interference represents a controlled sort of uncongenial control, not the normal variety

This gloss on the notion of non-arbitrary interference and control enables us to see why the republican tradition should only have indicted arbitrary interference, or the capacity for arbitrary interference, as the source of a restriction on someone's freedom. The story of Ulysses and the sirens would have served as an ancient illustration of the contrast in question. In republican thought, the distinction was important because of the institutional challenge it raised: that of identifying those conditions, if there are any, under which the governmental control of civic life can be rendered non-arbitrary and reconciled with the freedom of those who live under it. That challenge remains of contemporary significance.

Conclusion

Dahl's classic paper on power remains relevant and useful, then, in contemporary discussion. It may need some small amendments, as outlined in the first section. However, it allows of extensions that make room for both Marxist and civic republican perspectives on power. In addition, fleshed out with the distinctions between congenial and uncongenial power, and between the controlled and uncontrolled versions of uncongenial power, it enables us to reconstruct the republican conception of freedom. For a given choice, an agent enjoys such freedom to the extent that he or she is not subject to the uncongenial, uncontrolled power of others.

Republicans were particularly concerned with how people could be liberated from such power, not just in any choice, but in the basic liberties: in those choices that are of significance in personal life and that can be fully enjoyed by everyone consistently with being simultaneously enjoyed by others (Pettit 2008a). In order to explore the republican conception of liberty properly, then, we would need to move on to the consideration of the means whereby people might be protected in their basic liberties – and protected, if possible, by a state that exercised only a controlled version of uncongenial power in their lives. Nevertheless, that exploration would carry us well beyond the limited concerns of this paper.

Acknowledgements

The author thanks Casiano Hacker-Cordon and Mark Haugaard for comments on earlier drafts.

Notes

1. Notice that in this case, the distinction between possessing and exercising power tends to break down. To have the resources that enable A to exercise power will just be to exercise power, provided that A implicitly or explicitly invigilates B.
2. My inclination is to think that we should take an option to be a course of action such that, as things stand independently in the world, it is up to the agent whether or not that course of action materializes. This conception means that a course of action may be an option for me, even if it is not logically guaranteed

ROBERT A. DAHL

that I can realize it. All that is required is that in fact, things in the world conspire to let me realize it; they do not rule out that possibility, nor do they leave it just up to chance. It may be an option for me that I share a piece of information with someone, even though it is not logically guaranteed that he or she will hear what I say, but it will not be an option for me that I hit an archery target: things may or may not turn out to ensure that my effort is successful.

3. This scenario is effectively equivalent to one in which B succeeds in making interference by A unlikely by offering A rewards for not interfering. B will control A's interference but only in the congenial way that leaves A still with the interfering options that establish A's control.

4. In self-censorship B will seek to avoid z, in self-ingratiation B will seek to exploit A's taste for some reward, making the choice of z in the presence of that reward palatable to A.

5. Strictly, uncongenial initiatives that would normally impose such control will be sufficient to reduce freedom. See Pettit 2008b.

References

Bachrach, P. and Baratz, M., 1962. Two faces of power. *American Political Science Review,* 56, 947–952.

Dahl, R., 1957. The concept of power. *Behavioral Science,* 2, 201–215.

Dahl, R., 2002. Power (1968). In M. Haugaard, ed. *Power: A reader.* Manchester: Manchester University Press, 8–25.

Joyce, J.M., 1999. *The foundations of causal decision theory.* Cambridge: Cambridge University Press.

Lukes, S., 1974. *Power: A radical view.* London: Macmillan.

Maynor, J., 2003. *Republicanism in the modern world.* Cambridge: Polity Press.

Morriss, P,. 2002. *Power: A philosophical analysis, 2nd ed.* New York: Palgrave.

Nozick, R., 1969. Coercion. In P.S.S. Morgenbesser, M. White, eds. *Philosophy, science and method: Essays in honor of Ernest Nagel.* New York: St Martin's Press.

Pettit, P., 1997. *Republicanism: A theory of freedom and government.* Oxford: Oxford University Press.

Pettit, P., 2007. Republican liberty: Three axioms, four theorems. In C. Laborde and J. Manor, eds. *Republicanism and political theory.* Oxford: Blackwells.

Pettit, P., 2008a. The Basic Liberties. In M. Kramer, ed. *Essays on H.L.A. Hart.* Oxford: Oxford University Press.

Pettit, P., 2008b. Freedom and probability, *Philosophy and Public Affairs,* 36.

Richardson, H., 2002. *Democratic autonomy.* New York: Oxford University Press.

Skinner, Q., 1998. *Liberty before liberalism.* Cambridge: Cambridge University Press.

Viroli, M., 2002. *Republicanism.* New York: Hill and Wang.

Index

'actual and observable' conflict 57
advocate of democracy 83
American political science, behavioral revolution in 25
American Political Science Review 56
Annual Meeting of the American Political Science Association 54
apathetic majorities, role of 99

Baldwin, David 5
behavioral movement 2
behavioral revolution 26–7; in American political science 25
Benthamite principle 82
Bourdieu's conceptual vocabulary 6
British Labour Party 20

capitalism 20; socialism *vs.* 23
citizens, connections between leaders and 82–5
classical political theory 95
community power debate 53, 55–6, 58, 106
community power literature 56
community power theory 23
comprehensive paternalism 95
concept of competence, building on 85–6
concept of justice 109
'Concept of Power, The' 38, 39
conception of justice 109
congenial control, of power 120–1
Congress and Foreign Policy 3
controlled control, of power 121–2
Criterion of Competence 82, 89
Criterion of Economy 83
Criterion of Personal Choice 82

Dahl, Robert A.: analysis 118–19; compulsory power 64; concept and operational measure 108; concept of interests 113–14; 'concept of power' 54–5; concept *vs.* operational definition 61; concepts 21–4; and critics 53; as democrat 27–30; direct and immediate 65–6; extending Dahl's analysis 118–19; 'faces of power' 56–61; intellectual strengths of 11–12; last word of 108–14; legacy of 1–3;

material resources 65; misinterpretations 61, 105–8; on power 105–14; from power to freedom 119–22; preferences of *B* 61–2; proving it 25–7; questions 19–21; race and urban renewal treatment 15; research and teaching 12; as scholar, teacher, and democrat 11–18; subtlety, visibility, and awareness 64–5
Dahl–Lasswell difference 35
decision-making, levels of 41
delegation and control of leadership 75–7
democracy 8–9; and guardianship 87–8; and leadership 73–6, 79; Madisonian 97; management of 21; and polyarchy 46–8; procedural 95; shadow theory of 95; theoretical vision of 94; theorist of 29
Democracy and Its Critics 3, 98, 101
democratic decision-making process 3
democratic leadership 6
democratic political system 11–12, 16
democratic theory 3, 76, 97, 98
dominant social groups, role of 98

Equal Rights Amendment 100
equality *vs.* inequality 96
essential contestedness of concepts 109
essentialism 8
European Union 37

feminism: apathetic majorities, role of 99; classical political theory 95; comprehensive paternalism 95; dominant social groups, role of 98; Equal Rights Amendment 100; equality *vs.* inequality 96; full-dress political theory for women's movement 93; Madisonian democracy and 97; market capitalism 101; US political system 100; women's mobilization 94; women's rights in US Constitution 100
Foreign Affairs 1
forms of influence 39–40
Fourteenth Amendment 100

game theory 54
guardianship 75; democracy and 87–8

INDEX

'historical commitments' 24
Hochschild, Jennifer 3, 4
holistic concepts 21, 22
How Democratic is the American Constitution? 17

ideal-type concepts 6
Ignatieff, Michael 78
inequality, equality vs 96
influence: corporations 42; definition of 38;
    government and state 42; and interests 41–2;
    Journal of Political Power 42–4; levels of
    41–2; power and 110–11; treatment of 40
influence-centric phenomenon of politics 37
influence-wielders 40
interests, concept of 113–14
Isaac, Jeffrey 2

Johan Skytte Prize 1
Journal of Political Power 42–4
justice, concept of 109

Keohane, Nannerl O. 6

Lasswellian politics 35
leaders and citizens, connections between 82–5
leadership 6–7; concept of competence, building
    on 85–6; connections between leaders and
    other citizens 82–5; definition of 75; delegation
    and control 75–7; democracy and 73–5;
    guardianship, democracy and 87–8; as influence
    80–2; influence and ambiguity of 77–80
Lindblom, Charles E. 2, 19–20, 40
Lukes, Steven 56

MacKinnon, Catharine A. 7
Madisonian democracy 23, 97
market capitalism 101
Mayhew, David 4
Mill, John Stuart 83
mobilization, women 94, 101
Modern Political Analysis (*MPA*) 2, 5, 48–9;
    editions of 33; four-level framework in 41;
    influence and 'influence-terms' 38–44;
    major focus of 34; nature of politics 35–7;
    political systems, differences and
    similarities 44–8

national political systems 36, 44–7
nature of politics: *Modern Political Analysis*
    (*MPA*) (Dahl) 35–7; in New Haven 107
New Haven: nature of politics in 107; population
    in 15; 'socio-biological axis of race' in 14

On Political Equality 95
'one-dimensional view of power' 56–7, 62–3

parapolitics 36
persistent structural economic inequality 101

'pluralist concept of power' 55–6
pluralist democracy 107
'political influence' 43–4
'political power' 42–4
Political System, The (Easton) 35
political systems: democracy and polyarchy
    46–8; differences and similarities 44–8
politics 111; influence-centric phenomenon of 37
Politics, Economics, and Welfare 100
Politics: Who Gets What, When, How
    (Lasswell) 35
polyarchy 3, 4, 21, 22, 73, 75, 76, 84–6, 89;
    democracy and 46–8
'Polyarchal Democracy' 23
'Populist Democracy' 23
poverty, women's 101
power: amended Dahlian analysis of 116–18;
    congenial and uncongenial control 120–1;
    controlled and uncontrolled control 121–2;
    extending Dahl's analysis 118–19; and
    influence 110–11
Power: A Radical View (Lukes) 5, 59, 109
'power literature' 56
Preface to Democratic Theory, A 76
procedural democracy 95

racial hierarchy, issues of 17
radicalism 12
Rawls, John 109
Read, James H. 64
real-life democracies 4

sexual abuse 98
slavery, abolition of 17
small-D democracy 27–8
Social Contract (Rousseau) 83, 84
social psychology 54
socialism 20; *vs.* capitalism 23
'specialization of function' 80

'three-dimensional view of power' 57
'two-dimensional view of power' 57

uncongenial control, of power 120–1
uncontrolled control, of power 121–2
urban redevelopment 14–15
US Constitution, women's rights in 100
US political system 100

Weberian ideal types 6
Who Governs? 12–16, 20, 23–5, 29; research
    of 106–8
women: economic inequality 100; mobilization
    94, 101; movement, full-dress political theory
    for 93; poverty 101; rights in US Constitution
    100; wages and hours, regulation of 99

'zero-sum concept of power' 63–4